What Was The American Dream? And What Happened To It?

Lynn Atwell

GodsPurposes.org

The Author has tried to show due diligence in every area of grammar, spelling, punctuation, wording, and Scripture notation. If however, in the course of your reading, you find any errors or suggestions to improve this text, it will be gratefully appreciated. Email: "webmaster@GodsPurposes.org.

This booklet is available in any quantities at cost. Contact the author by email at "webmaster@GodsPurposes.org".

This author did not obtain the endorsement, nor does he have any connection with any of the sources quoted in this text. He does not claim to represent their views, nor does he claim their agreement with his. Whatever brief quotations that have been used are by the 'fair use' provisions of the copyright act.

Scripture quotations are from the King James Version Bible.

Front Cover Art is John Trumbull's (1817-1843) *Declaration of Independence*

Special acknowledgment is given to those men and women of faith in my life who were witnesses to me of the truth, and who interceded to God on my behalf that He might open my eyes to see Christ.

Copyright © 2012 Lynn Atwell
All rights reserved.
ISBN-10: 1475094620
ISBN-13: 978-1475094626
Printed in the USA

TABLE OF CONTENTS

1. The Present State of America 1

2. What Was the American Dream? 8

3. The Changing Focus of the American Dream 17

4. How the Changing Focus of the "Dream" Affected American Life 26

5. The High Cost of America's False Dreams 36

6. What is the Future of America? 48

7. What Can Be Done to Restore the Dream? 55

Many of the financial figures quoted in this text have become antiquated, and should not be used for any current factual data. In most cases these figures are now far worse than when this text was written; but in any case they are only presented to give credence to what is presented in this essay.

The Author

The Present State of America

Babylon, Greece, Rome, France, Great Britain—what do these former world empires have in common with the United States of America? They were all super powers who lost their position in the world because they collapsed from within. At the zenith of their power they were unconquerable; but, because of moral excesses, they were either overthrown, or greatly diminished to a position of weakness among the nations. Are we right to say that America is among these former empires, and is now becoming a second rate power? The signs of America's collapse are undeniable. Economically, morally, and spiritually, we have already become bankrupt. Only our military superiority sustains our image to the world as a super power; but even that is an economic burden that we can not shoulder much longer.

Financially, America is broke. Our national debt is such an insurmountable amount, that there is no way that it can be repaid by the present means of taxation. The Federal deficit, along with future obligations to Social Security, Medicaid, Federal Pensions, Military Pensions, and other social programs, now stands at 65 trillion dollars, and exceeds the Gross Domestic Product of the entire world.[1] To understand the significance of this amount, every individual—man, woman, and child—in this country, would have to repay $216,000.00 to settle this debt. Most people cannot dig themselves out of their own debt, much less try to repay what our government owes; and this does not even take into consideration the debt of the individual states that are also bleeding red ink. California's debt alone is now at forty-two billion dollars.[2] On top of the Federal and state debts, are all the corporate debts that are

---

[1] Jerome R. Corsi, © 2009 WorldNetDaily, www.worldnetdaily.com/index.php?fa=PAGE.view&pageId=88851
[2] © USA Today, http://www.usatoday.com/news/nation/2009-01-15-schwarzenegger-california-deficit_N.htm

owed by American businesses, banks, and insurance companies; and, when we add in the debts of individuals and families—credit cards, car loans, mortgages, etc—we can readily see that we have dug ourselves into a deep pit.

We might ask ourselves, 'How did we get into this financial mess?' The answer is as simple, or as complex as you want to make it. On the simpler side someone has said, "If your outgo exceeds your income, then your upkeep will be your downfall." We, as Americans, started spending more than we could afford. Instead of living within our means, we mortgaged the future of America by our over-indulgent spending; and we created a tidal wave of debt that is about to sweep us away. We borrowed against our children's future so that we might enjoy unprecedented prosperity. Since the days of Franklin Roosevelt, when, in an effort to deliver America from the Great Depression, many of the great "social" programs were enacted, we have lavishly spent money on wasteful government bureaucracies, welfare giveaways, entitlements, and pork legislation; but as Barack Obama recently said in a speech, "The party's over."

While many have praised Federal programs such as "The New Deal," "The Great Society," Social Security, and Medicare, few people understood the costs that these policies would ultimately exact upon the American people. Even the present government bailouts, which are efforts to restore our economy, are only more wasteful giveaways that are sinking us deeper in debt. Furthermore, America's military involvement in wars and conflicts around the world, have been at a tremendous cost. While some of these efforts may have been necessary to preserve our freedom, many were not. Much of the "Cold War" spending was totally unnecessary. Some annalists have estimated that America spent over thirteen trillion dollars[3] to defend ourselves against a Soviet threat that was largely over-

---

[3] Center For Defense Information,
http://www.cdi.org/Issues/milspend.html

estimated. Viet Nam and Iraq are both wars which have cost thousands of American lives and billions of dollars; but the purposes for our involvement in them is unclear, and the end result has been disastrous.

Greed and corruption within our government has also led to much of our national debt. Pork legislation, federal bureaucracies, salaries and pensions for congressmen have reached the level of absurd. Much of the spending that comes from Washington is only for the purpose of the self-enrichment of those who hold office, or their bureaucratic counterparts. Many people who are elected have high ideals when they go to Washington, but are soon corrupted by the atmosphere that prevails there. Like the British missionaries who went to Hawaii to "do well", and did "very well," many of our elected officials use their office for personal gain. Their only political agenda is how to get re-elected. The "party" atmosphere in Washington reminds us of the indulgences of the courts of King Louis XVI of France, just before the French revolution.

Corporation spending has also been excessive, and for many companies disastrous. Many companies have been run like small monarchies, with the CEO acting as the king. Gross salaries and bonuses, employee trips and parties, and other "perks" that have been handed out, have robbed the coffers of many companies. Large corporations have gobbled up smaller companies, only to steal what assets those companies may have had. Small businesses, run by hard-working Americans, have been destroyed by the aggressive tactics of the "super" stores, whose only concern is their bottom line profit. Americans have invested billions of dollars into the stock of these corporations, only to see their nest eggs wither away by the falling stock market. Powerful banks, which merged together with investment firms, swallowed up smaller banks, and now are on the verge of bankruptcy. Only the bailout money of the Federal government sustains them from failing completely. Hedge funds, exotic investments, and the crooks of Wall Street have all contributed to the multi-billion dollar losses of the companies for which many people work, and depend upon for their living.

Individuals and families have done no better. Many people, lured by the availability of easy credit, have over-extended their borrowing to the point where they cannot pay their bills. Credit card spending, buying expensive houses and cars, exotic vacations, and other excesses by consumers have left many to file bankruptcy. Many families struggle to pay for all of this borrowing by having two wage earners working night and day. Now, many people are out of jobs, the result of down-sizing and the economic slow down. College students, who borrowed money to pay tuition, and ran up credit card debt to pay for expenses, struggle to find the jobs that they prepared for. Most college degrees are now useless pieces of paper, with those who earned them having no outlet for their training. Even those graduates, who may find work, struggle to repay the mountain of debt that was accumulated.

As honest people struggle to make a living, the dark side of America has seen the rise of violent street gangs. The Mexican drug cartels, Russian mafia, biker gangs, Los Angelus street gangs, and a host of other groups, who are feeding on America's lust for pleasure, are flourishing. Our present immigration polices, and lack of enforcement, has opened the flood gates to illegal aliens, whose only purpose has been to take advantage of the freedom we have here in America, and exploit our weaknesses. These gangs have become so entrenched in our country that our law enforcement people cannot effectively deal with them. Their violent actions, powerful weaponry, and the sheer number of the members of these gangs, are a force to be reckoned with. It would take military intervention by the armed forces of this country to even begin to root them out; but of course, our liberal laws and courts would never allow such actions.

White collar crime has also flourished in America, as unscrupulous people have taken advantage of the huge amount of investment dollars that have been flowing, and the lack of oversight thereof. The investment world has been shocked time and again with the discovery of yet more fraudulent schemes. Companies, such as Enron, have bilked investors and employees out billions of dollars. A significant number of penny stocks are nothing more than elaborate hoaxes run by mafias. They drive up the price of their stocks by issuing glamorous reports, and then sell out, leaving investors with worthless stock certificates. The latest, and possibly the worst investment scandal ever, that of Bernard Madoff, purportedly has cost investors upwards of fifty billion dollars. His Ponzi scheme existed in the plain sight of regulators, who failed to give even basic oversight to his investment company.

Adding to these higher profile crimes are those which have begun to plague every area of American life. While there have always been certain neighborhoods where no one was safe, even in daylight hours, we now see the tentacles of violence and crime spreading in every part of America. Drug dealing, theft, sexual assaults, and murder take place in even the "safest" areas of our land. School violence has struck in even the most upscale communities. Adding to these more "common" crimes has been the rise of identity theft, where thieves use the personal information of others to steal wealth electronically. Scam artists steal millions from unsuspecting Americans, particularly those who can least afford it—the poor and elderly.

Corporate downsizing, recession or depression (whatever you call it), and a host of other economic setbacks have put millions of Americans out of work. In some of the hardest hit states, unemployment is close to ten percent[4], while the

---

[4] ©CNN Money.com,
http://money.cnn.com/pf/features/lists/state_unemployment/

national rate is over 7 percent, a 15-year high[5]. Because of this, more and more people are looking for any way to make money, and are not adverse to use illegal and immoral means to acquire it. The loss of American jobs is driving many people to desperation, and to do things which they would not otherwise commit. Robbery, fraud, internet schemes, gambling activities, Ponzi schemes, and other "easy" methods to make money are on the increase by ordinary citizenry.

As with Rome, America's hedonistic culture, where any lifestyle is acceptable, is at the root of our destruction. Our society is now a moral swampland, where every kind of immorality is acceptable—as long as people mutually consent, it's ok. Pre-martial sex, extra-marital sex, and perverse sex, which once drew the condemnation of society, are now openly practiced without the least amount of attention. American companies now give to non-traditional marriages the same benefits as those who follow God's intended purpose. Is it any wonder American companies are failing when they promote these unbiblical lifestyles? Daytime television, with its steamy soap operas, and nighttime situation comedies, where nothing is sacred and sexual innuendoes are the main script, flood our minds with immoral thoughts. Adult movies, pornography on the magazine rack and internet, the portrayal of casual sex by Hollywood, have all led to the moral corruption of society. Sex education is freely taught in schools, while any teaching about God or morality is denied.

The last element of America's collapse, and the one which is the most profound, is the spiritual. Although our constitution openly professes our founding father's belief in God; the Bill of Rights insures our freedom of religion; our Pledge of Allegiance declares that we are "one nation under God"; and printed on our money is "In God We Trust"; the majority of

---

[5] Bureau of Labor Statistics.

Americans live as if there is no God. Liberal influences and court decisions have banned any teaching related to God from public schools. Creationism is forbidden to be taught, and anything but restricted "student led" prayer is excluded. While forty percent of Americans, who are polled, "say" that they regularly attend church, actual head counting belies that figure. Most people view Sunday as their day for relaxing, not a day of worship. Most disturbing is the disinterest of America's youth in spiritual matters—little wonder when they are bombarded in schools with humanism and evolution. Only those youth, who have strong religious upbringing and church going parents, are likely to show any spiritual interest.

While we once considered ourselves to be a "Christian" nation, now, every religion and god is wholly accepted as being part of our "multi-cultural" society. Common religious bonds, which once fashioned the philosophy of American life, now are deemed "narrow-minded" by the liberal planners in our colleges and government. Even among the church-going, religious faction of American society there has been a "falling away" from Biblical principles. We have traded sound teaching and doctrine for being entertained in church. To go along with the "party" atmosphere of American culture, we now have the "feel good" religion of the "health, wealth, and happiness" gospel. Although many mainline denominations have long ago abandoned Biblical truth, even among those who consider themselves to be "Bible believing" there has been a growing perversion toward "easy believism", worldliness, and humanism. What we have left in our churches are many "professing", but few genuine converts to Christ; we have preaching and teaching that accommodates anyone's lifestyle; and we have an emotional, man-centered worship that glorifies the creature instead of the creator.

What Was the American Dream?

There are many modern ideas about what is the "American Dream." Some view it as owning your own home. Others view it as the opportunity to become financially wealthy. Still others say it is the freedom to do whatever you want, and to become whatever you would like to be—even the President of the United States. If those are the ideals that most people embrace as the American Dream, than for many, the dream has become a nightmare.

Home foreclosures have reached near record levels, and the number of homeowners who are "underwater"[6] is nearly fourteen million[7]. However, those people are among the group that can even afford to purchase a house. Many people never even get out of the rut of paying rent and being able to buy a home of their own. Even many elderly, who own their homes after many years of payments, find that they must sell them, or do a "reverse mortgage"[8] in order to pay for living expenses and property taxes. Because of property tax laws, high utility costs, and Medicare regulations[9], many elderly are forced to either sell, or have their homes foreclosed upon. Furthermore, the "freedom" in owning a home is not all that it portends to be. Many communities have such restrictive zoning laws and building regulations, that most people are forbidden to do anything but the most basic upkeep on their houses. Some cities require homeowners to have permits to even paint their house, or do any other minor repairs. While many people, of

---

[6] The term used to describe the condition of owing more than a house is worth.
[7] © The New York Times, http://www.nytimes.com/2009/05/04/opinion/04mon2.html
[8] The term used to describe the process of a person mortgaging their home and drawing upon the equity to pay for living expenses.
[9] Before a person can use Medicare to pay for a nursing home, they must first liquidate all assets, including their house, and all proceeds are given to the state.

days gone by, used their homes for business or professional proposes, such is not permitted with today's zoning laws. Many cities now require licenses and fees to even have a garage sale. Considering all of the stress of paying for a home and property taxes; and with all the restrictive laws and regulations prohibiting what people can do with, and in their homes; it can hardly be imagined that this is the American Dream.

The recent fall of the stock markets due to recession, the bursting of the "tech bubble,"[10] the panic selloff after September 11th, and other forces have all but dashed the "dreams" of many Americans to become rich. The dream of enjoying a comfortable retirement, with millions of dollars in their nest eggs, is all but gone for most average Americans, who have seen their IRAs plummet in value over the last several years. Even before recent events, the Federal Government, through taxation and regulation, has made the dream of becoming wealthy almost unreachable for most people. There have been a few niche entrepreneurs, like Bill Gates, who have amassed a fortune in recent years; but the tax laws that have been passed since the early 1900's have only served to protect those who already made their fortunes, and effectively shut-out the average person from becoming wealthy. Most people are taxed just to the point of having enough to live on, with nothing left over to invest or start a business. Even if a person somehow manages to start a business or company, complicated Federal income and Social Security tax laws, OSHA regulations, EPA regulations, state and local unemployment and business taxes, fire, health, and business regulations, all effectively discourage and prevent most people from enjoying their own business and becoming wealthy. Many new businesses fail within the first two years, and most do not make it past five. The reasons: paperwork, taxes, and regulations all but kill their incentive, and consume

---

[10] The term used to describe the past astronomical rise in value of technology companies and their stock prices.

what little profit people may earn. There is simply too much work for too little reward in owning a business; and most people give up, or go broke trying. While many Americans "dream" of working for themselves and enjoying the fruits of their labors, the majority will find that the way to financial independence has been effectively blocked off to them. For many, the only financial "dream" left to them is to win a state controlled lottery, or engage in criminal activity.

While some may argue that it is still possible for anyone to become President, realistically, most modern day elections are manipulated and controlled. In the twentieth century there have been very few "Abe Lincoln" type presidents, who rose to that office on their own ability and strength of character. Unless a person is wealthy enough to finance their own campaign, have family ties to political insiders, or be chosen and groomed for higher office by a major party, there is little chance that a "common" man will ever again be elected to that office. Even to become a Senator or Representative requires tremendous financial backing and support from the election "machines."[11]

Howbeit, aside from political office, are not American's free to become whatever they wish? To some degree they are. However, even certain fields, such as medical doctors, are extremely difficult to enter without having some "insider's" pull to get a person into medical college. To go to a prestigious business or law school, such as Harvard or Yale, also requires family or insider assistance, not to mention huge financial resources. These Ivy League colleges are the "prerequisite" for many important business, legal, political, and professional positions; and those who are not among societies "upper crust" will find it difficult to be accepted to them. Most Americans are relegated to "middle class" occupations, and will find it very hard to break into the "higher rungs" of business or society.

---

[11] The term used to describe the political organizations who control which candidates run for office on their tickets.

America, like the French royal court before the revolution, has become a nation of "elites." America has become a nation that is controlled by those who are wealthy and have political clout; and the frequency of those who break through the "glass ceiling" to fulfill their "dreams" is extremely low. Unless someone is fortunate enough to be talented in sports or entertainment, be opportunistic or inventive, most people will find that their "real" opportunities are very limited.

While these "dreams" are the "carrots" which are dangled before the masses of the American people, and those who want to live here, for most of us, that is all they are. While some people still may fantasize about having power and wealth, most Americans are resigned to live modestly, and have lost all hope of becoming rich and famous. Some people are cynical about life in America, but the majority has learned to be content with their status. The difference between those who are contented and those who are not is—what "dream" are they satisfied with. Those who futilely struggle after the, almost unattainable, "dreams" that have been falsely set before them, will only become discouraged and bitter. Nonetheless, there is a "dream" which is still quite attainable for all of us. It is the "dream" which brought the Pilgrims to the shores of America, and that which our Founding Fathers guaranteed when they wrote the Constitution and the Bill of Rights.

However, before exploring what the "real" American Dream is, we must ask the following questions: What conditions provoked the first Europeans to leave "civilized" society and come to a continent that was an unsettled wilderness? Why would people risk their lives to cross the ocean and come to a place that was largely unknown, and filled with dangers? While some came for adventure, and others came to make their fortune, most of those who first came, came for other reasons. What, therefore, was life like in the seventeenth and eighteenth century for most people who lived in Europe? First of all, nearly every country was ruled by a monarch and an accompanying "royal" class. This was made up of princes and princesses, dukes and duchesses, lords and ladies, and other individuals considered to be the "upper," or ruling class of those societies. These were not individuals who rose to their positions by intelligence or hard work, but simply were born into their place of wealth and power. They were deemed to be of "royal" blood; and therefore were "destined" by God to be in control of the "inferior" masses. Secondly, nearly all land and business was owned or controlled by those of the royal class. Most people either worked directly for, or as tenants of those in control. Becoming independent, wealthy, or owning property was nearly impossible for most common people. Thirdly, there were no basic human rights—laws were always in favor of the ruling class; courts were always biased against the commoner; and therefore, injustices toward the common man abounded. Lastly, and most intolerable, was that even the personal beliefs of the people were controlled by state religions. There were only state controlled churches, which were presided over by appointed priests, bishops, pastors, and others, who were under the direct control of the ruling class, or, the equally powerful, "state church." The rule of the Roman Catholic Church was the most dominate force in organized religion; and later, the Church of England became the state church of Great Britain. The freedom of religion, as we know it today, was non-existent; and those who tried to worship God according to their own dictates, were often killed, tortured, imprisoned, or lost their means of livelihood.

What this atmosphere bred was a desire for liberty that motivated people to seek a way out of the oppressive conditions under which they lived. The "dream" that these first settlers had in coming to America was of a new life. A life where, yes, they would have the freedom to own property and have a better standard of living; but more importantly, a life where they would have the same basic rights as everyman, and be treated fairly according to just laws and courts; and, most importantly, a life where they could worship their Creator God according to truth and their own conscience. While the original Pilgrims still owed allegiance to the monarchs of the Old World, and many of the original colonies were formed under the authority and guidance of their European rulers, they found in America a foretaste of those freedoms that would later come to fruition in the Declaration of Independence, the United States Constitution, and the Bill of Rights. They found in America an opportunity to cast away the old systems and restraints that kept people in servitude to their king, their masters, and the state church.

What is important to realize however, is that these people did not come here to live without any restraints. These original settlers were not of those who merely wanted the liberty to live as they pleased. Most of the early Pilgrims were very religious people, who understood the importance of government and freedom "under God." They understood that men, as individuals, or society as a whole, cannot enjoy true freedom and liberty unless they are controlled by the belief in, and a personal, reverential fear of God. They also believed that God established human government for the good of mankind; and that anarchy and rebellion against authority would only bring chaos. Most of those who came still believed in loyalty to their European monarchs, and the governors that were appointed to rule over them. It was only when these "foreign" authorities began to make life in America as intolerable as it had been in Europe that the idea of a free and independent country became the "dream" of the masses.

Declaration of Independence

When in the Course of human events it becomes necessary for one people to dissolve the political bands which have connected them with another and to assume among the powers of the earth, the separate and equal station to which the Laws of Nature and of Nature's God entitle them, a decent respect to the opinions of mankind requires that they should declare the causes which impel them to the separation.

We hold these truths to be self-evident, that all men are created equal, that they are endowed by their Creator with certain unalienable Rights, that among these are Life, Liberty and the pursuit of Happiness. — That to secure these rights, Governments are instituted among Men, deriving their just powers from the consent of the governed, — That whenever any Form of Government becomes destructive of these ends, it is the Right of the People to alter or to abolish it, and to institute new Government, laying its foundation on such principles and organizing its powers in such form, as to them shall seem most likely to effect their Safety and Happiness. Prudence, indeed, will dictate that Governments long established should not be changed for light and transient causes; and accordingly all experience hath shewn that mankind are more disposed to suffer, while evils are sufferable than to right themselves by abolishing the forms to which they are accustomed. But when a long train of abuses and usurpations, pursuing invariably the same Object evinces a design to reduce them under absolute Despotism, it is their right, it is their duty, to throw off such Government, and to provide new Guards for their future security. — Such has been the patient sufferance of these Colonies; and such is now the necessity which constrains them to alter their former Systems of Government.

The American Dream, that dominated the consciousness of our country for almost two hundred years, was that men have the right, under God, to live in liberty and freedom. That men, as individuals, *"are endowed by their Creator with certain unalienable Rights, that among these are Life, Liberty and the pursuit of Happiness."*[12] It was the dream that men ought to be at liberty to worship God, not by the dictates of a state religion, but according to God's revealed truth. The primary focus of the dream was not to become rich, or become politically powerful—they had already tasted what the abuse of power led to; but that men ought to be free, within reasonable restraints, to do, or to become what they so desired. The dream was that our central government would only be established to protect the personal liberties of its citizenry, and not to dictate how they should live. The personal liberties, found in the Bill of

---

[12] Declaration of Independence

Rights, made it plain which liberties were to be guaranteed, and restricted the government from overstepping its authority. The founding fathers were so concerned about the abuse of power, that it included the provision that people have a right to bear arms—not for the purpose of sport or hunting, as some would have us believe; but to protect themselves from an abusive government that threatened personal liberties.

Hubert Humphrey — *"Certainly one of the chief guarantees of freedom under any government, no matter how popular and respected, is the right of the citizens to keep and bear arms. This is not to say that firearms should not be carefully used and that definite safety rules of precaution should not be taught and enforced. But the right of the citizens to bear arms is just one guarantee against arbitrary government and one more safeguard against a tyranny which now appears remote in America, but which historically has proved to be always possible."*

Bill of Rights

Amendment I

Congress shall make no law respecting an establishment of religion, or prohibiting the free exercise thereof; or abridging the freedom of speech, or of the press; or the right of the people peaceably to assemble, and to petition the Government for a redress of grievances.

Amendment II

A well regulated Militia, being necessary to the security of a free State, the right of the people to keep and bear Arms, shall not be infringed.

Amendment III

No Soldier shall, in time of peace be quartered in any house, without the consent of the Owner, nor in time of war, but in a manner to be prescribed by law.

Amendment IV

The right of the people to be secure in their persons, houses, papers, and effects, against unreasonable searches and seizures, shall not be violated, and no Warrants shall issue, but upon probable cause, supported by Oath or affirmation, and particularly describing the place to be searched, and the persons or things to be seized.

Amendment V

No person shall be held to answer for a capital, or otherwise infamous crime, unless on a presentment or indictment of a Grand Jury, except in cases arising in the land or naval forces, or in the Militia, when in actual service in time of War or public danger; nor shall any person be subject for the same offence to be twice put in jeopardy of life or limb; nor shall be compelled in any criminal case to be a witness against himself, nor be deprived of life, liberty, or property, without due process of law; nor shall private property be taken for public use, without just compensation.

Amendment VI

In all criminal prosecutions, the accused shall enjoy the right to a speedy and public trial, by an impartial jury of the State and district wherein the crime shall have been committed, which district shall have been previously ascertained by law, and to be informed of the nature and cause of the accusation; to be confronted with the witnesses against him; to have compulsory process for obtaining witnesses in his favor, and to have the Assistance of Counsel for his defence.

Amendment VII

In Suits at common law, where the value in controversy shall exceed twenty dollars, the right of trial by jury shall be preserved, and no fact tried by a jury, shall be otherwise re-examined in any Court of the United States, than according to the rules of the common law.

Amendment VIII

Excessive bail shall not be required, nor excessive fines imposed, nor cruel and unusual punishments inflicted.

Amendment IX

The enumeration in the Constitution, of certain rights, shall not be construed to deny or disparage others retained by the people.

Amendment X

The powers not delegated to the United States by the Constitution, nor prohibited by it to the States, are reserved to the States respectively, or to the people.

The Changing Focus of the American Dream

The question that we now raise is, 'How did the dream of the first European settlers in America, which was the simple desire for freedom and liberty under God, come to mean something different?' While some would argue that the dream has never changed, the focus of our modern society is certainly different than that of our forefathers. While their belief was in the Sovereign God, only under whose wings[13] man could enjoy freedom, today's concept of the American Dream has changed from that belief to a humanistic viewpoint. It has been a slow transition to be sure, but it has brought about a complete change in American society and culture. Consider the following quotes from throughout the history of America.

The First Charter of Virginia, granted by King James I, on April 10, 1606—"*We, greatly commending, and graciously accepting of, their Desires for the Furtherance of so noble a Work, which may, by the Providence of Almighty God, hereafter tend to the Glory of his Divine Majesty, in propagating of Christian Religion to such People, as yet live in Darkness and miserable Ignorance of the true Knowledge and Worship of God...*"

The Mayflower Compact, authored by William Bradford, 1620— "*Having undertaken, for the glory of God, and advancement of the Christian faith, and honor of our King and Country, a voyage to plant the first colony in the northern parts of Virginia, do by these presents solemnly and mutually, in the presence of God, and one of another, covenant and combine our selves together…*"

Patrick Henry, May 1765—"*It cannot be emphasized too clearly and too often that this nation was founded, not by religionists, but by Christians; not on religion, but on the gospel of Jesus Christ. For this very reason, peoples of other faiths have been afforded asylum, prosperity, and freedom of worship here.*"

---

[13] Psalms 36:7, Psalm 57:1, Psalm 91:4

The Declaration of Independence, July 4, 1776—*"We hold these truths to be self-evident, that all men are created equal, that they are endowed by their Creator with certain unalienable Rights, that among these are Life, Liberty and the pursuit of Happiness."*

James Madison, 1778—*"We have staked the whole future of American civilization, not upon the power of government, far from it. We've staked the future of all our political institutions upon our capacity…to sustain ourselves according to the Ten Commandments of God."*

Thomas Jefferson, 1781—*"God who gave us life gave us liberty. And can the liberties of a nation be thought secure when we have removed their only firm basis, a conviction in the minds of the people that these liberties are of the Gift of God? That they are not to be violated but with His wrath? Indeed, I tremble for my country when I reflect that God is just; that His justice cannot sleep forever."*

George Washington, June 8, 1783—*"I now make it my earnest prayer the God would have you and the State over which you preside, in His holy protection, that he would incline the hearts of the citizens to cultivate a spirit of subordination and obedience to government; to entertain a brotherly affection and love for one another, for their fellow citizens of the United States at large, and particularly for their brethren who have served in the field; and, finally, that he would be most graciously pleased to dispose us all to do justice, to love mercy, and to demean ourselves with that charity, humility, and pacific temper of mind, which were the characteristics of the Divine Author of our blessed religion, and without an humble imitation of whose example in these things we can never hope to be a happy nation."*

James Madison, June 20, 1785—*"Religion is the basis and Foundation of Government."*

Benjamin Franklin, 1787 —*"Here is my Creed. I believe in God, the Creator of the Universe. That He governs it by His Providence. That He ought to be worshipped."*

Benjamin Franklin, 1787 —*"God governs in the affairs of man. And if a sparrow cannot fall to the ground without his notice, is it probable that an empire can rise without His aid? We have been assured in the Sacred Writings that except the Lord build the house, they labor in vain that build it. I firmly believe this. I also believe that, without His concurring aid, we shall succeed in this political building no better than the builders of Babel"*

James Madison, March 4, 1809—*"We have all been encouraged to feel in the guardianship and guidance of that Almighty Being, whose power regulates the destiny of nations."*

John Adams, June 28, 1813—*"The general principles on which the fathers achieved independence were. . . . the general principles of Christianity. . . . I will avow that I then believed, and now believe, that those general principles of Christianity are as eternal and immutable as the existence and attributes of God; and that those principles of liberty are as unalterable as human nature."*

Abraham Lincoln, September 11, 1858—*"Our reliance is in the love of liberty which God has planted in our bosoms. Our defense is in the preservation of the spirit which prizes liberty as the heritage of all men, in all lands, everywhere."*

Grover Cleveland, circa 1885—*"A government for the people must depend for its success on the intelligence, the morality, the justice, and the interest of the people themselves."*

Woodrow Wilson, circa 1913—*"Liberty has never come from Government. Liberty has always come from the subjects of it. The history of liberty is a history of limitations of governmental power, not the increase of it."*

Herbert Hoover, circa 1929—*"A splendid storehouse of integrity and freedom has been bequeathed to us by our forefathers. In this day of confusion, of peril to liberty, our high duty is to see that this storehouse is not robbed of its contents."*

James Truslow Adams, 1931, the term, "American Dream," was first used in his book, *The Epic of America*—*"The American Dream is that dream of a land in which life should be better and richer and fuller for everyone, with opportunity for each according to ability or achievement. It is a difficult dream for the European upper classes to interpret adequately, and too many of us ourselves have grown weary and mistrustful of it. It is not a dream of motor cars and high wages merely, but a dream of social order in which each man and each woman shall be able to attain to the fullest stature of which they are innately capable, and be recognized by others for what they are, regardless of the fortuitous circumstances of birth or position."*

Franklin Roosevelt, circa 1944—*"Democracy cannot succeed unless those who express their choice are prepared to choose wisely. The real safeguard of democracy, therefore, is education."*

Franklin Roosevelt, circa 1944— *"The only sure bulwark of continuing liberty is a government strong enough to protect the interests of the people, and a people strong enough and well enough informed to maintain its sovereign control over the government."*

Dwight D. Eisenhower, circa 1953—*"There is nothing wrong with America that the faith, love of freedom, intelligence and energy of her citizens cannot cure."*

John F. Kennedy, circa 1961—*"Our problems are man-made, therefore they may be solved by man. And man can be as big as he wants. No problem of human destiny is beyond human beings."*

Gerald Ford, May 31, 1976—*"In the two centuries that have passed since 1776, millions upon millions of Americans have worked and taken up arms, when necessary, to make the American dream a reality. We can be proud of what they have accomplished. Today, we are the world's oldest republic. We are at peace. Our nation and our way of life endure. And we are free."*

Bill Clinton, Nov 4, 1992—*"We need to empower our people so they can take more responsibility for their own lives in a world that is ever smaller, where everyone counts. We need a new spirit of community, a sense that we are all in this together, or the American Dream will continue to wither. Our destiny is bound up with the destiny of every other American."*

Wikipedia®, May 12, 2009—*"The American Dream refers to the freedom that allows all citizens and all residents of the United States to pursue their goals in life through hard work and free choice. The American Dream often refers to the opportunity for immigrants to achieve greater material prosperity than was possible in their countries of origin. America has been viewed as a land in which one's prospects in life are defined by one's talents and energy rather than by one's family wealth or political connections."*

What is necessary to see, from the preceding quotes, is the very perceivable drift from the belief that God gives and sustains liberty, to the idea that men, through their own devices and systems, create and sustain their own liberty. What the change in the American Dream has been, is that we have attributed the dream to the principles of democratic government, education, and our own resolve to be free; and that it has been brought about by the efforts of the American people, past and present. Furthermore, while we are not debating the religious beliefs or affiliations of the sources which we quote—some of those who understood from Whom the well-spring of liberty comes, may have been non-religious; and those who gave a humanistic slant to the source of liberty, may themselves have been very pious— what is plan is the subtle change in American thought. It is the change from a dependence upon God to the belief that men must maintain, through human efforts, their own freedom and liberty.

Well might we ask, what bought about this change of philosophy? The steps that America has followed to its inevitable destruction, are the same as those outlined in the book of Romans.

Romans 1:18-25, 28 For the wrath of God is revealed from heaven against all ungodliness and unrighteousness of men, who hold the truth in unrighteousness; Because that which may be known of God is manifest in them; for God hath shewed it unto them. For the invisible things of him from the creation of the world are clearly seen, being understood by the things that are made, even his eternal power and Godhead; so that they are without excuse:

Because that, when they knew God, they glorified him not as God, neither were thankful; but became vain in their imaginations, and their foolish heart was darkened. Professing themselves to be wise, they became fools, And changed the glory of the uncorruptible God into an image made like to corruptible man, and to birds, and fourfooted beasts, and creeping things. Who changed the truth of God into a lie, and worshipped and served the creature more than the Creator, who is blessed for ever. Amen. And even as they did not like to retain God in their knowledge, God gave them over to a reprobate mind, to do those things which are not convenient;

1. America began to forget. We forgot the feudal conditions under which our ancestors lived for centuries. When our forefathers came to this continent they tasted a breath of freedom that was only dreamed about in the old world. For the first hundred years or so of our existence the memories of that former life was still emblazoned upon the minds of the people. Even as the first pilgrims began to die off, the stories they had told to their children and grand-children kept the reality of what they had experienced alive upon the minds of the following generations. However, as the years began to separate us from those pioneers, so did our appreciation for true liberty begin to wane. Moreover, we began to forget that it was God who established our forefathers in this land. When once the struggle for freedom was over, our remembrance of God's mercy began to dim. Most Americans today have no idea of how the faith of our founders was what gave them the courage and fortitude to leave their homelands and come to America; and how that faith strengthened them to endure the hardships that lay ahead.

Daniel Webster—"*Finally, let us not forget the religious character of our origin. Our fathers were brought hither by their high veneration for the Christian religion. They journeyed by its light, and labored in its hope. They sought to incorporate its principles with the elements of their society, and to diffuse its influence through all their institutions, civil, political, or literary."*

2. America became unthankful. The tendency of most people, who never experience the sufferings and hardships of life, is to be unthankful for what they have. Most Americans today take for granted what our forefathers only dreamed about. Many of them suffered and died to secure for us the liberties which we enjoy, while most Americans express little appreciation for them. Furthermore, and most importantly, we began to be unthankful to the God whose providence brought our forefathers to this shore, and endowed them with the ideals of true freedom and liberty. Those who ventured to this distant shore were keenly aware that God's hand had brought them here, and they were diligent to offer Him the praise and thanksgiving He deserved. Thanksgiving Day has changed from a time when we reflect upon God's goodness and give Him praise, to that of feasting and praising the gods of football and shopping.

George Washington—*"It is the duty of all Nations to acknowledge the providence of Almighty God, to obey his will, to be grateful for his benefits, and humbly to implore his protection and favor."*

Samuel Adams—*"It is therefore recommended ... to set apart Thursday the eighteenth day of December next, for solemn thanksgiving and praise, that with one heart and one voice the good people may express the grateful feelings of their hearts and consecrate themselves to the service of their divine benefactor"* (First Official Thanksgiving Proclamation)

3. America became proud. Instead of continuing to look to God as the author and sustainer of our liberty, we began to look to human efforts and institutions. Instead of giving God the glory for what He has done for us, we began to attribute freedom to our own doing. Even our history books have been humanized to reflect the changing philosophy of our country. When in times past children were taught about the influence which faith in God had upon our early settlers, now, nearly all mention of God is deleted and forbidden in the classroom.

Today, everyone is a "hero," and God receives hardly any honor at all in our nation. Now, everything that happens is attributed to either natural forces or human efforts. Those who do attempt to glorify God in our country are belittled and scoffed at. Television, Hollywood, Universities, and our own government has painted the picture that faith in God is only a "crutch" for the weak-minded; and that the "educated," "scientific," "up to date" view of our world is that our universe is the result of the "Big Bang"; life is the result of evolutionary forces; and man is his own god, and is responsible for his own destiny.

Abraham Lincoln—*"We have been the recipients of the choicest bounties of heaven. We have been preserved, these many years, in peace and prosperity. We have grown in numbers, wealth and power, as no other nation has ever grown. But we have forgotten God. We have forgotten the gracious hand which preserved us in peace, and multiplied and enriched and strengthened us; and we have vainly imagined, in the deceitfulness of our hearts, that all these blessings were produced by some superior wisdom and virtue of our own. Intoxicated with unbroken success, we have become too self-sufficient to feel the necessity of redeeming and preserving grace, too proud to pray to the God that made us! It behooves us, then to humble ourselves before the offended Power, to confess our national sins, and to pray for clemency and forgiveness."*[14]

4. America became foolish. The Scriptures declare, **"The fear of the LORD is the beginning of knowledge: but fools despise wisdom and instruction."**[15] When America turned its heart from trusting in God, and seeking His face for wisdom and guidance, and instead looked to its own strength and wisdom, our downfall was determined. Those who first came to America were devout and earnest in seeking God's protection and guidance. Those who framed the Constitution also showed great diligence to ask for God's wisdom and direction in laying the cornerstone of our new nation. Now,

---

[14] Abraham Lincoln's 1863 Thanksgiving Proclamation
[15] Proverbs 1:7

most of those who sit in Congress scoff at the idea that we need God, or should pray to God. We now have "experts," trained in humanistic universities, that have all the answers to our problems.

James Garfield—*"We can not overestimate the fervent love of liberty, the intelligent courage, and the sum of common sense with which our fathers made the great experiment of self-government."*

5. America became imprudent. When men turn their back on God, God, in return, gives **"them over to a reprobate mind, to do those things which are not convenient."** Please note that the Scripture does not say that God causes, or brings about our foolish decisions—He merely lets us have our own way. When America, as a whole, began to think we didn't need God, but we became "wise" enough to make our own choices, we were doomed as a nation. Soon to follow were extravagant, wasteful spending programs by our government; and a populace that was eager for free handouts. The government sponsored "party" had begun, but the real American Dream was over. **"There is a way which seemeth right unto a man, but the end thereof are the ways of death."**[16]

Ronald Reagan—*"Government can't solve the problem. Government IS the problem."*

Stephen Grover Cleveland—*"It is the responsibility of the citizens to support their government. It is not the responsibility of the government to support its citizens."*

Warren G. Harding—*"Our most dangerous tendency is to expect too much of government, and at the same time do for it too little."*

---

[16] Proverbs 14:12

How the Changing Focus of the "Dream" Affected American Life

As with almost every human endeavor, the ideals, ambitions, and zeal of a new venture are never better than when they start out. Most changes to an entity—be it a person, company, organization, or country—that cause its eventual destruction, are made because of human depravation. Our forefathers went through a great struggle to establish this nation. It was clear to them that the ideals of freedom and liberty were a gift of God. It was also clear that God's hand had allowed them to persevere and win their struggle for freedom. In framing the foundation of our new government—the Constitution and Bill of Rights—they sought God's face in asking for wisdom and protection. Almost every law of our new nation was patterned after the commandments of God found in the Bible. In the beginning of our history there was no "separation of church and state" such as we see today. Religion and government walked hand in hand in the establishment of our country.

The first amendment to the Constitution, known as the First Article in the Bill of Rights, did not restrict the role of religion in government; but forbade the suppression of religion, and the establishment of a state controlled religion. In proclaiming that *"Congress shall make no law respecting an establishment of religion, or prohibiting the free exercise thereof,"* it was made clear that individuals were to have complete freedom to worship God according to the dictates of their own conscience. It was also made clear that the place of religion in our society was not to be suppressed. What this amendment dictated was that government was not to get involved in matters of religion; but we see just the opposite of that taking place today. The purpose and meaning of that article has been so perverted by our courts, that we now have numerous laws enacted that are directly against the individual's freedom of religion, and the establishment of the philosophy of "freedom from religion" that so dominates our country. We now have embedded in our government, and in our educational system the religion of humanism; and it is a religion that has been established by the laws of our country and the courts of our country. It is a religion that is protected from all opposition, and is supported by the taxes of the American people. Humanism, along with its siblings, "Big Bang" and "Evolution," now is the official "religion" of America, and dominates every aspect of our national life.

Ronald Reagan—*"There is a fundamental difference between separation of church and state and denying the spiritual heritage of this country. Inscribed on the Jefferson Memorial in Washington, DC are Jefferson's words, 'The God Who gave us life gave us liberty -- can the liberties of a nation be secure when we have removed a conviction that these liberties are the gift of God?' "*

These changes to our country did not come overnight however. The trampling of our liberties by big government would never have been permitted in its early years; and any attempt to thrust God from our country and establish a state religion would have been met with violent actions. We have been the "frog slowly cooked to its death" over the past two hundred years. What began as a sincere effort to have God and His Word be the cornerstone of our nation's foundation, slowly evolved into what we see today. What happened to America is what happened to ancient Israel. After going through all the struggles to enter the Promised Land; and then conquering all their enemies once they entered the Land; they forgot the God who had led them out of Egyptian bondage and gave them the victory over all their enemies. They soon turned their hearts away from God as they began to enjoy the "land flowing with milk and honey."

James Madison—*"I believe there are more instances of the abridgement of the freedom of the people by gradual and silent encroachments of those in power than by violent and sudden usurpations."*

Exodus 3:7-8 And the LORD said, I have surely seen the affliction of my people which are in Egypt, and have heard their cry by reason of their taskmasters; for I know their sorrows; And I am come down to deliver them out of the hand of the Egyptians, and to bring them up out of that land unto a good land and a large, unto a land flowing with milk and honey; unto the place of the Canaanites, and the Hittites, and the Amorites, and the Perizzites, and the Hivites, and the Jebusites.

Judges 2:7-12 And the people served the LORD all the days of Joshua, and all the days of the elders that outlived Joshua, who had seen all the great works of the LORD, that he did for Israel. And Joshua the son of Nun, the servant of the LORD, died, being an hundred and ten years old. And they buried him in the border of his inheritance in Timnath-heres, in the mount of Ephraim, on the north side of the hill Gaash. And also all that generation were gathered unto their fathers: and there arose another generation after them, which knew not the LORD, nor yet the works which he had done for Israel. And the children of Israel did evil in the sight of the LORD, and served Baalim: And they forsook the LORD God of their fathers, which brought them out of the land of Egypt, and followed other gods, of the gods of the people that were round about them, and bowed themselves unto them, and provoked the LORD to anger.

Our forefathers also discovered that America was **"a land flowing with milk and honey."** In America they not only found freedom and independence from their European oppressors, but they also found that this land was rich in beauty and natural resources. Men cannot be faulted for wanting to make a living and developing the resources that God gives to them—indeed, they are commanded by God to do so. The problem with most men however, is that they turn their hearts away from the Living God, who blesses them with all things, to the gods of materialism and self-reliance. The liberties that men found in America provided the prospect for making great wealth, and along with it, power. This country not only provided the opportunities for the average man to own property and make a living, but for men such as Carnegie, Rockefeller, Vanderbilt, and Morgan to exploit these liberties for their own selfish ambitions. Greed and lust for power soon began to replace love for God and brotherly kindness.

Gen 2:15 And the LORD God took the man, and put him into the garden of Eden to dress it and to keep it.

1 Timothy 6:9-10 But they that will be rich fall into temptation and a snare, and into many foolish and hurtful lusts, which drown men in destruction and perdition. For the love of money is the root of all evil: which while some coveted after, they have erred from the faith, and pierced themselves through with many sorrows.

As more and more people abandoned their zeal for God and His Word, so also we see the changing focus of the true American Dream. While America remained "religious" well into the twentieth century, those believers considered to be fundamental[17] soon became a minority. The primary shift in philosophy, from that of honoring the God who gave us liberty, to that of materialism and humanism, soon began to erode the foundations laid down by our founding fathers. When men trade the True and Living God for idols of wood, metal, and stone, even so they also become receptive to false teaching and ideas. Consequently, the measuring stick for many of our laws was no longer the Word of God, but how the obtaining and protection of wealth could be propagated. Those men who had obtained great fortunes soon began to unduly influence our elected leaders by intimidation and bribery. These barons began to introduce into our legal system laws that

---

[17] By fundamental we mean a strict adherence to the teachings of God's Word.

protected their wealth, and at the same time made it increasingly harder for the average man to obtain it. Foundations, trusts, and legalized tax loopholes provided these men and their descendents with the shelters that protected their fortunes; and the graduated income tax, business taxes, social security taxes, and a myriad of other taxes and regulations made it difficult, not only to start a business, but to make a living with it.

Jeremiah 2:11-13 Hath a nation changed their gods, which are yet no gods? But my people have changed their glory for that which doth not profit. Be astonished, O ye heavens, at this, and be horribly afraid, be ye very desolate, saith the LORD. For my people have committed two evils; they have forsaken me the fountain of living waters, and hewed them out cisterns, broken cisterns, that can hold no water.

The start of the twentieth century in America also saw the rise of the mega-corporations. Although foreign corporations, such as the British East India Company, had existed for over a hundred years before the American Revolution, early Americans had seen the evils of that form of enterprise, and made these kinds of business arrangements difficult to form. Early settlers practiced the Biblical ideal of family farms, family practices, and family businesses. This economic model gave early America its small town, family orientated, community atmosphere, and provided almost everyone a source of adequate income. However, all of that was to change as New Jersey, and then Delaware liberalized their laws to make corporations easier to form—all for the benefit of raising tax money for those states. Other states soon followed and corporations began to proliferate. While many small corporations existed in the late nineteen hundreds, that also was to change. The liberalizing of laws also led to corporate consolidation. It is estimated that from 1898 to 1904, eighteen hundred U.S. corporations were consolidated into one hundred-fifty-seven.[18] Small companies found themselves either making sweetheart deals to sell out, or were the victims of hostile takeovers. The nineteen seventies saw the advent of the corporate raiders. These were companies or groups of individuals who would leverage the purchase of larger, profitable corporations, and then sell or mortgage the valuable assets for profit, leaving the former company to flounder in debt, and many filing for bankruptcy.

What, may we ask, are the evils of corporations, and why does the Bible condemn them?

• Corporations are soulless institutions, whose only aim is to make more profit. The driving principles are only those which bolster the stock price. They only benefit American communities when they can use benevolence to bolster their public image.

• Although corporations provide jobs where they are located, they generally have destroyed small town America. Families and small businesses cannot compete against these large behemoths that use their leverage to run smaller companies out of business. Consider what happens when a mega-store moves into a community.

• The jobs that most corporations provide are mostly menial, low paying occupations for those who are employed by them. Most workers find themselves in repetitious, boring work with no incentive to be productive. Only the top management, who often live like kings, and the rich stockholders are the true beneficiaries.

• Corporations live and grow by gobbling up smaller companies, and soon find themselves drowning in debt. They become so large that many can no longer be effectively managed, and fall victim to insider fraud and pilfering. In order to present a positive balance sheet to stockholders, many use

---

[18] Wikipedia ©, http://en.wikipedia.org/wiki/Corporation

questionable accounting and outright lies about their state of business. The American investment community has been shocked again and again by the likes of WorldCom, Adelphia, and Enron; and we now see the need for large government bailouts to support the likes of General Motors, Chrysler, insurance companies, investment firms, and the large mega-banks.

Isaiah 5:8 Woe unto them that join house to house, that lay field to field, till there be no place, that they may be placed alone in the midst of the earth!

The nineteen hundreds also saw the disappearance of many family farms that were once the basis of rural life in America. Government intrusion into farming practices, regulations, increasing costs, and the lure of "good paying" factory jobs, all led many people to abandon farming and move to the cities. Many of those farms that did remain are either large family owned or corporate farms. This migration from country life to city life had a great impact on American philosophy and culture. The close knit family structure, simple, basic farm life, and the rural communities they supported, were all traded for the material pursuits of life.

Micah 4:4 But they shall sit every man under his vine and under his fig tree; and none shall make them afraid: for the mouth of the LORD of hosts hath spoken it.

As America turned more and more to the gods of humanism and materialism, it produced an explosion in the number of laws and regulations. When men turn from God, who is the author and sustainer of liberty, and attempt to maintain their own freedom apart from God, they must do so by the enacting of laws—which effectively robs them of their liberties. This is because men, who will not be governed by God, must be controlled by outward restraints. Contrary to popular beliefs, man is not inherently good; but rather, man is a fallen creature subject to sin; and sin must be restrained. Furthermore, as the evils of materialism and greed began to abound, so did the need for more laws to protect society. By comparison, the number of laws that governed ancient Israel (given to them by God in the Old Testament) was six hundred-thirteen[19]; and many of those are dietary and ceremonial, not moral or ethical laws. The Ten Commandments was the most basic and necessary set of edicts that could, if followed, provide for a peaceful society. The exact number of laws that we live under in the United States is almost incalculable—because of all the different Federal, State, and Local jurisdictions. Some would guess that the number is in the hundred's of thousands. However, if we include all of the Federal governmental agencies and their regulations (OHSA, EPA, HUD, ATF, etc), plus all the regulations of state and local agencies, the number would well be in the millions. Although some of our laws are patterned after God's Word, most are the product of our changing philosophy.

1 Timothy 1:9-10 Knowing this, that the law is not made for a righteous man, but for the lawless and disobedient, for the ungodly and for sinners, for unholy and profane, for murderers of fathers and murderers of mothers, for manslayers, For whoremongers, for them that defile themselves with mankind, for menstealers, for liars, for perjured persons, and if there be any other thing that is contrary to sound doctrine;

Gal 5:13 For, brethren, ye have been called unto liberty; only use not liberty for an occasion to the flesh, but by love serve one another. For all the law is fulfilled in one word, even in this; Thou shalt love thy neighbour as thyself.

What we now find in America is that almost every aspect of our lives is controlled by external laws and regulations. Americans no longer live in a "free" country, but are in bondage to a restrictive governmental and legal system.

---

[19] http://www.jewfaq.org/613.htm

America's legislative bodies, law enforcement personnel, lawyers, judges, and regulatory inspectors are the enforcers for the new "ruling class" in our land. Every American is under the watchful eye of "big brother's" law enforcement personnel, who are empowered to imprison, fine, and control the citizenry. A person cannot make a living, work on their home, build a fire, or do anything that should be considered as part of their *"unalienable rights"*—which are *"Life, Liberty and the pursuit of Happiness,"*[20]—without being subject to some law or regulation, and under the oversight of some government official. As an example we now have "garage sale police," who drive around making sure everyone is in compliance by having permits and following regulations. Common sense and inventive thinking are both muffled, because we are no longer free to express ourselves, except within the bounds of a complex system of laws.

John F. Kennedy—*"Conformity is the jailer of freedom and the enemy of growth."*

Furthermore, our spirit of adventure and exploration is severely limited. Everywhere we go we are told to "keep out", "no hunting", "no fishing", "no trespassing", and "restricted area". Even our "so-called" National and State Parks have so many restrictions and regulations that people do not have the freedom to explore or enjoy themselves without worrying whether they are breaking some law. Most areas are off limits, and in many parks people are restricted to man-made trails with the threat of fines for stepping off of them. Activities such as camping, fishing, hiking, canoeing and many others are not allowed except by permit. Of course all of these restrictions are done in the name of "environmental" concerns. The only ones free to do as they please are the government officials and park personnel, while the tax payers, who funded these areas, are restricted. Even children, who need to be encouraged to

---

[20] Declaration of Independence

explore, exercise, and show imagination, are everywhere told "no skateboarding," "no ball playing," "no trail bikes," "no swimming," and a myriad of other restrictions.

Along with restricting personal liberties, all of these laws have severely limited American industry's ability to compete. Not being able to hire the most competent workers, or to fire incompetent workers, advancement of less qualified personal because of race or gender consideration, have forced many companies to struggle with workers who are unqualified or less qualified than others. Civil Rights legislation, American's With Disabilities legislation, and other social legislation have taken away the freedom of businesses to structure themselves to be productive and profitable. These laws have also been the reason for a rising cynicism among those who get passed over, despite their hard work and qualifications. Regulations concerning workplace safety, regulations brought about by environmental concerns, unemployment taxes, social security taxes, and a myriad of other taxes and regulations have all contributed to making it unprofitable for companies to manufacture products in America. These are some of the reasons why we have seen such a vast exodus of companies to other countries to produce their goods. We are not suggesting that all of these laws are without some merit, or that some companies exploited workers and the environment in their quest for greater profits, but many of these "laws" are against common sense and allow no flexibility. A great amount of time and money is wasted just to satisfy these regulations without providing any added benefits. All of these laws and regulations could effectively have been avoided if men acted in the fear of God, and with love and respect for their fellow man.

The High Cost of America's False "Dreams"

Along with the burgeoning expansion of our legal system came the necessity for an ever ballooning governmental workforce—to "make sure" everyone is in compliance with all of the laws and regulations. Federal law enforcement agencies such as the FBI, DEA, ATF, EPA, U.S. Marshals, IRS, OSHA, and many other enforcement divisions employ thousands of workers. Along with those who are directly involved in enforcement are the tens of thousands of bureaucrats who must insure that all of the paperwork and processes involved with carrying out government programs and laws is maintained. Along with federal enforcement personnel and bureaucrats, we have similar structures at the state and local levels. It is estimated that there are over seventeen thousand[21] law enforcement agencies throughout the United States, with many overlapping jurisdictions and duplication of services. Furthermore, we now have an overburdened court system that must handle the cases of those who act contrary to these laws. Judges, prosecutors, defense attorneys, court personnel, and other supporting personnel, must channel the millions of defendants through the legal system. At the end of the chain is the prison system and its personnel, who oversee those deemed worthy of incarceration for their misdeeds. While many convicts are violent offenders that society needs to be protected from, some are merely tax evaders, those convicted of petty crimes, smalltime drug users and sellers, and other offenders, who could be dealt with in better ways. The total number of government personnel at all levels is now estimated to be close to twenty million.[22]   Americans now work almost seven months out of the year to pay for the cost of all government

---

[21] FBI, http://www.fbi.gov/ucr/ucr.htm
[22] Data 360 ©,
http://www.data360.org/dsg.aspx?Data_Set_Group_Id=228

personnel and programs; and the Federal government itself consumes forty percent of the gross domestic product.[23]

America has followed ancient Israel by abandoning its faith in God, and we have reaped the consequences. God warned Israel what would happen to them when they wanted an earthly king to rule over them, instead of being ruled by God. (Please note that the cost of Israel's king was only going to be ten percent of their income, while in America the cost has risen far above that.)

1 Samuel 8:4-22 Then all the elders of Israel gathered themselves together, and came to Samuel unto Ramah, And said unto him, Behold, thou art old, and thy sons walk not in thy ways: now make us a king to judge us like all the nations. But the thing displeased Samuel, when they said, Give us a king to judge us. And Samuel prayed unto the LORD. And the LORD said unto Samuel, Hearken unto the voice of the people in all that they say unto thee: for they have not rejected thee, but they have rejected me, that I should not reign over them. According to all the works which they have done since the day that I brought them up out of Egypt even unto this day, wherewith they have forsaken me, and served other gods, so do they also unto thee. Now therefore hearken unto their voice: howbeit yet protest solemnly unto them, and shew them the manner of the king that shall reign over them. And Samuel told all the words of the LORD unto the people that asked of him a king. And he said, This will be the manner of the king that shall reign over you: He will take your sons, and appoint them for himself, for his chariots, and to be his horsemen; and some shall run before his chariots. And he will appoint him captains over thousands, and captains over fifties; and will set them to ear his ground, and to reap his harvest, and to make his

---

[23] Rep. Ron Paul of Texas,
http://www.lewrockwell.com/paul/paul117.html

instruments of war, and instruments of his chariots. And he will take your daughters to be confectionaries, and to be cooks, and to be bakers. And he will take your fields, and your vineyards, and your oliveyards, even the best of them, and give them to his servants. And he will take the tenth of your seed, and of your vineyards, and give to his officers, and to his servants. And he will take your menservants, and your maidservants, and your goodliest young men, and your asses, and put them to his work. He will take the tenth of your sheep: and ye shall be his servants. And ye shall cry out in that day because of your king which ye shall have chosen you; and the LORD will not hear you in that day. Nevertheless the people refused to obey the voice of Samuel; and they said, Nay; but we will have a king over us; That we also may be like all the nations; and that our king may judge us, and go out before us, and fight our battles. And Samuel heard all the words of the people, and he rehearsed them in the ears of the LORD. And the LORD said to Samuel, Hearken unto their voice, and make them a king. And Samuel said unto the men of Israel, Go ye every man unto his city.

Along with the size and cost of big government has come the dependence of many Americans upon the government to support them. When Americans began to abandon their trust in God, and in His provisions for their lives, many looked to the government to supply their needs. The excesses of the roaring twenties brought about the great depression of the thirties; but instead of bringing about a national repentance towards God, and seeking His blessing once more, our country was lured into thinking that the great social programs would save us. The first of those programs was the New Deal, brought about by the Franklin Roosevelt administration. Among many programs that were instituted were the Civil Works Administration (CCW), Federal Emergency Relief Act (FERA), Public Works Administration (PWA), Works Progress

Administration (WPA), and the biggest "Ponzi"[24] scheme of all time—Social Security. Although many liberal minded Americans praised these efforts, they were only the beginning of the great Federal government "money pit" that is now swallowing up all of America's resources. While many people temporarily benefited from these programs, no one envisioned the ultimate cost that they would exact upon our economy. Though many liberals attributed these programs with delivering us from the Great Depression, that was more the result of our involvement in World War II then in these social programs.

Another massive government program was the Great Society, instituted by the Lyndon Johnson administration. During that time this country saw the passage of the Civil Rights Acts of 1964 and 1968. Although the Bible certainly condemns **"respect of persons,"**[25] this is a matter of personal morality, and not legislated social engineering. The liberalization of the immigration laws, with the passage of the Immigration and Nationality Act of 1965, opened the floodgates to those immigrants who dramatically changed the philosophical landscape of America. Also, during this period, America's future was further mortgaged by the institution of Medicare and Medicaid, programs that the government cannot manage nor afford. Liberalization of the welfare system also saw the introduction of Food Stamps and other government "handout" programs that rewarded non-work and immoral lifestyles. America's Christian heritage was further attacked by the institution of many liberal, national endowments for the arts, "sciences," and education: among these are the Public Broadcasting System (PBS), National Endowments for the Arts, and National Endowments for the Humanities. These

---

[24] An investment scheme named after Charles Ponzi whereby older investors are paid returns with the funds from newer investors, and not from any actual earnings of the enterprise.

[25] James 2:1 My brethren, have not the faith of our Lord Jesus Christ, the Lord of glory, with respect of persons.

programs all drip with socialistic, humanistic, evolutionistic propaganda, and most are blatantly anti-Christian.

What has been the result of all these "social" programs upon the American economy and lifestyle?

• We have created a bureaucratic monstrosity in Washington and in our state capitols. There has been added layer upon layer of people who are employed just to administer these programs. We have a significant workforce in our country that do nothing to add to our economy, but rather are leeches upon it. They do not produce anything that adds to our gross domestic product, but rather, through taxation, they and the programs they oversee, are sucking the life's blood out of America. We now live in an era when almost fifty percent of the population either works for the government, or are the recipients of its handouts. Is it any wonder that we see such a surge of liberalism in our country? Liberal proponents have used the hard-working taxpayer's money to buy elections through these, and other humanistic programs. Are we suggesting that every government job is unnecessary?— no. There are legitimate functions of government that should be maintained, but not on the level that we see today.

Gerald Ford—"*A government big enough to give you everything you want is a government big enough to take from you everything you have.*"

• We have created a philosophy in America that the government owes its people a living, regardless of whether they work for it or not. We have people who do nothing but live off of welfare; people who do jobs that have no material benefits, but are supported through government grants; and people who expect the government to bail them out of every adverse situation, regardless of how they got into it. It is the great demise of democracy that the majority can reward themselves with benefits for which they have not justly earned. Our forefathers had it right when they limited those who had the right to vote. Now, we have made it effortless for every derelict, junkie, alcoholic, and deadbeat to vote themselves government assistance by electing socialistic liberals to government office.

John Kennedy—"*And so my fellow Americans, ask not what your country can do for you; ask what you can do for your country.*"

John Q. Adams—"*Always vote for principle, though you may vote alone, and you may cherish the sweetest reflection that your vote is never lost.*"

• We have created a great cynicism in our country among those who believe in working for a living and reaping the rewards of one's personal achievements. Honest, hardworking Americans have been made to shoulder the burden of big government and the social giveaway programs. There is no greater source of discontent among industrious people than the amount of taxes they are forced to pay, and the wasteful government spending of their tax dollars. We are reaching the point where many people are giving up, and either hide their earnings, or become a part of the problem by accepting the giveaways. It is becoming an accepted norm that it's ok to cheat or be a deadbeat, because everybody is doing it.

Teddy Roosevelt— "*The Roman Republic fell, not because of the ambition of Caesar or Augustus, but because it had already long ceased to be in any real sense a republic at all. When the sturdy Roman plebeian, who lived by his own labor, who voted without reward according to his own convictions, and who with his fellows formed in war the terrible Roman legion, had been changed into an idle creature who craved nothing in life save the gratification of a thirst for vapid excitement, who was fed by the state, and who directly or indirectly sold his vote to the highest bidder, then the end of the republic was at hand, and nothing could save it. The laws were the same as they had been, but the people behind the laws had changed, and so the laws counted for nothing.*"

• Even with the high amount of taxes that are exacted upon those who work, we keep falling farther behind in our efforts to support these programs. America's national debt is the evidence that we simply cannot afford to sustain these social programs. Furthermore, our industrial base has been eroded because of the high costs of doing business in America, and we have less people, with decent paying jobs, to bare the costs of big government. We have almost reached the point of no return of ever being able to pay off, or even reduce our debt; and because the majority of American's are benefiting from the government programs, it is becoming politically impossible to make the drastic changes necessary to stop the bleeding.

Franklin Pierce—"*The revenue of the country, levied almost insensibly to the taxpayer, goes on from year to year, increasing beyond either the interests or the prospective wants of the Government.*"

As America lost its dependence upon God for our provisions, we also lost our dependence upon Him for protection. Our forefathers were keenly aware of their need for God to fight their battles and to protect them. They were a small group of pioneers compared to the armies of their European oppressors; and they were ill-trained and armed to fight for their independence, and to stand among the nations of the world. As God did for ancient Israel, it was He who established them upon this continent and gave them victory over their enemies. However, even as Israel abandoned her faith in God and started to trust in the arm of the flesh (Egypt), even so America has fallen into the same error. Our government now spends close to one trillion dollars annually[26] for all defense related programs. The United States is perhaps the most militarily powerful nation that has ever existed, and yet, following World War II, we have seen either defeat or stalemate in every major confrontation since then. America lost its first war in the jungles of Viet Nam because we had neither the willingness, nor the determination to win. We have the most sophisticated weaponry and intelligence systems ever devised, and yet all that failed us in the terrorist's attacks of September 11th. We have dazzled the world with our "high

---

[26] Wikipedia ©,
http://en.wikipedia.org/wiki/Military_budget_of_the_United_States

tech" missiles, tanks, helicopters, jet fighters, drones, and other "star wars" weaponry, and yet we cannot defeat the likes of Osama bin Laden, the Taliban, the Islamic Jihad, and other terrorist groups armed with only rifles and roadside bombs. We have become like the once unconquerable Roman Empire, which crumbled from within due to its moral excesses and pagan beliefs. America once stood for God and righteousness, and has been the defender of many just causes throughout the world. Now, we are immoral and corrupt, and use our military power only to protect our commercial interests throughout the world.

Benjamin Harrison—"*We Americans have no commission from God to police the world.*"

Deuteronomy 7:7-8 The LORD did not set his love upon you, nor choose you, because ye were more in number than any people; for ye were the fewest of all people: But because the LORD loved you, and because he would keep the oath which he had sworn unto your fathers, hath the LORD brought you out with a mighty hand, and redeemed you out of the house of bondmen, from the hand of Pharaoh king of Egypt.

Deuteronomy 20:1-4 When thou goest out to battle against thine enemies, and seest horses, and chariots, and a people more than thou, be not afraid of them: for the LORD thy God is with thee, which brought thee up out of the land of Egypt. And it shall be, when ye are come nigh unto the battle, that the priest shall approach and speak unto the people, And shall say unto them, Hear, O Israel, ye approach this day unto battle against your enemies: let not your hearts faint, fear not, and do not tremble, neither be ye terrified because of them; For the LORD your God is he that goeth with you, to fight for you against your enemies, to save you.

Psalm 20:6-8 Now know I that the LORD saveth his anointed; he will hear him from his holy heaven with the

saving strength of his right hand. Some trust in chariots, and some in horses: but we will remember the name of the LORD our God. They are brought down and fallen: but we are risen, and stand upright.

Psalm 108:12-13 Give us help from trouble: for vain is the help of man. Through God we shall do valiantly: for he it is that shall tread down our enemies.

Isaiah 31:1 Woe to them that go down to Egypt for help; and stay on horses, and trust in chariots, because they are many; and in horsemen, because they are very strong; but they look not unto the Holy One of Israel, neither seek the LORD!

When America turned from God to the idols of humanism and materialism, it also lost many of His benefits. One of the most significant was that of God's provision for the health of His people. Although the Bible certainly advocates healing and health through proper diet and herbal remedies, the major emphasis is on faith and prayer—concepts that are far from the minds of most people. America now has the largest and most technologically advanced system of medical care in the world. Many of the larger hospital\universities are like small cities in both size and the number of people that they employ and service; but we rank among the lowest nations in terms of our actual health—our rate of obesity, diabetes, heart conditions, cancer, and many other diseases are among the highest in the world. Along with this burgeoning health care system has come the tremendous cost of maintaining it. We now have a medical system that is so expensive that the majority of Americans cannot afford it. The cost of medical insurance is so high that individuals cannot pay the premiums; and companies who offer health care benefits to their workers are being dragged down by the cost. All of this has come about because our focus has changed from God, **"who healeth all thy diseases,"** to trust in our own resources.

Psalm 103:2-3 Bless the LORD, O my soul, and forget not all his benefits: Who forgiveth all thine iniquities; who healeth all thy diseases;

James 5:14-16 Is any sick among you? Let him call for the elders of the church; and let them pray over him, anointing him with oil in the name of the Lord: And the prayer of faith shall save the sick, and the Lord shall raise him up; and if he have committed sins, they shall be forgiven him. Confess your faults one to another, and pray one for another, that ye may be healed. The effectual fervent prayer of a righteous man availeth much.

Because of the Federal Government's "blank check" mentality, we dole out billions of dollars in grants and entitlements, "pork" spending, and support of useless programs that offer no significant payback. Many colleges and universities receive enormous sums of money just to do research on senseless "scientific" study. Long term senators and representatives insure their re-election by a constant flow of federal money toward their states in the form of "project" spending that is wasteful and unnecessary. Many federal programs exist only for the self-sustainment of those who are the administrators and employees of those programs. One of America's great "white elephants" has been the space program. Untold billions of dollars has been spent, all for the purpose of discovering the "origin of the universe" and finding life outside of our planet. This country could have saved vast sums of money and resources if only we believed what our fore-fathers did—**"In the beginning God created the heaven and the earth."**[27]

One of the key instruments that has been used to turn America's focus from God to that of humanism has been to change the philosophy of America's education system. While almost all schools started out as being church affiliated early in our countries history, and almost all textbooks based their

---

[27] Genesis 1:1

teachings on the Bible, that has all changed with the advent of the public schools, the infiltration of teachers and professors who are blatantly anti-Christian, and the introduction of the evolutionistic-humanistic textbooks that we see so prominently today. From a system that once molded the character of our children and pointed them to a faith in God, we now witness a deliberate, organized effort to erase the memory of God and morality from the minds of our youth. Many of the prominent colleges in America—Princeton, Yale, Harvard, and many others—all began with God-honoring ideals, but have now digressed into institutions which undermine the faith of their students. Those who masterminded the changing focus of the American Dream saw that the battleground of their attack must be in the arena of higher education. Their aim was to supplant the faith of our fathers by infiltrating the colleges and universities with teachers and professors who promoted the liberal, humanistic doctrines that we see so dominate today. These colleges in turn would turn out school teachers, lawyers, and other professionals that had been indoctrinated in the humanistic philosophy.

Now, through the misinterpretation of the Constitution, and other liberal court decisions, any teachings about God, Creationism, Bible-based morality, or the use of prayer are all deemed illegal in our public schools. Instead, we have the religion of secular humanism practiced, evolution presented as fact without any rebuttal, and sex-education taught to our children. Sex outside of marriage is condoned, contraceptives are passed out, and abortion counseling is provided. Many of our inner-city schools are like war zones, where discipline is non-existent, and the atmosphere needed for learning is far from conducive. When we told God to leave our schools and disregarded the teachings of His Word, the void that resulted has been replaced by a disregard for human life and a return to a hedonistic lifestyle in our youth. In recent years we have witnessed an increasing amount of school violence, drug use, and pre-martial sex even among grade school children. Despite the fact that we have the best educational facilities that American debt can provide, we rank among the lowest civilized countries in terms of actual learning. We have wasted the minds of our children, and created a generation of youth that is violent, and has no fear of God or authority. We have sown to the wind in minds of our youth, and we are about to reap the whirlwind.

Psalm 36:1 The transgression of the wicked saith within my heart, that there is no fear of God before his eyes.

Hosea 8:7 For they have sown the wind, and they shall reap the whirlwind: it hath no stalk: the bud shall yield no meal: if so be it yield, the strangers shall swallow it up.

The majority of Americans have traded their faith in God for trust in other things—government, health care, military might, education, and money. From almost a total reliance upon God in the early years of our country, we have come to the place where every effort is being made to banish the idea of God from our society. Americans have become self-sufficient, no longer needing God or His blessings. Like the church of Laodicea, which prophetically pictures the end of the church age, Americans have become **"rich, and increased with goods, and have need of nothing."** Instead of trusting in the God of our Fathers, we now give praise to the gods which we have created—the pseudo "America Dream," democracy, humanism, and materialism. However, we are beginning to discover that we are **"wretched, and miserable, and poor, and blind, and naked."**

Revelation 3:17 Because thou sayest, I am rich, and increased with goods, and have need of nothing; and knowest not that thou art wretched, and miserable, and poor, and blind, and naked:

What is the Future of America?

The next question that must be pondered is—what will be the future state of America if drastic changes are not made? Let us first of all examine America's economic outlook. While we continue to show some semblance of order and soundness, the underlying truth is that America is already bankrupt. We only continue to function because we still have good credit in the eyes of the world, and our lifestyle is being financed by more and more borrowing. While once Americans winced at any kind of budget shortfalls, now, most people seem unconcerned about the trillions in debt that this country has amassed. Many Americans are so concerned about what they can get from the government, that they fail to see our eminent collapse. Instead of dealing with the root causes of our problems, we continue to believe that the federal government can bail us out with more spending. While we have already discussed why we may have passed the point of no return, we must now question what is the prognosis for our country.

Admittedly, much of our debt is owed to the American people themselves in terms of Social Security and Medicare obligations, Federal and military pensions, and other future promissory entitlements. The cancellation of these obligations could, and would be the first steps in the event of a monetary meltdown. While millions of Americans would suffer from such a loss, there may be no other workable solutions. Now, while these "promissory" entitlements are the bulk of America's indebtedness, the current level of "hard" debt, which has already been borrowed and spent, is around eleven trillion dollars.[28] This debt is backed by various kinds of securities—Savings Bonds, Treasury Bonds, and other kinds of notes promising future payment. These bonds and notes also have attached to them the promise to pay a certain rate of interest on top of the principle borrowed, when repaid. The

---

[28] 2010 figures

interest due last year on these debts was over four hundred billion dollars.[29] These debts are growing because year after year we fail to balance our budget, and must borrow more and more to finance our overspending. The servicing of the interest itself, now consumes a major portion of our tax dollars.

Much of this debt is also owed to the American people: Insurance companies, banks, state and local governments, pension funds, and Savings Bond owners, hold approximately three trillion dollars worth of our debt.[30] The Federal Reserve and Inter-governmental Holdings, such as money owed to the Social Security Trust Fund, is around five trillion dollars.[31] The rest of our indebtedness is owed to foreign governments, with Russia, Brazil, China, Japan, the Middle Eastern countries, and the United Kingdom holding the bulk.[32] While again, we could default on our debts to American lenders, foreign debt holders present a bigger problem—unless, like America has often done for poor countries, we are merely forgiven; but that is not likely to happen. What is more likely is that our collapse will drag the rest of the world into financial chaos as well.

As we have already discussed, drastic measures to balance our budget are not politically viable, because liberal office holders are too concerned about their own re-election to make any hard decisions. Also, those who are dependant upon the government for their livelihood—government employees and those who receive the benefits—are almost a majority in this country. Added to that are the millions of Americans who are legitimately owed benefits—Social Security recipients, bond holders, and military and government pensioners. These people are not going to be receptive to having their pensions and nest eggs defaulted upon, and will join those who will resist any attempt to stop the bleeding. Therefore, we may conclude, that

---

[29] http://www.treasurydirect.gov/govt/reports/ir/ir_expense.htm
[30] http://www.globalshift.org/2010/02/06/who-owns-the-u-s-debt/
[31] Ibid
[32] Ibid

although there may be some small bandages applied to our hemorrhaging, they will not be effective enough to prevent our financial demise.

The first evidence of our collapse will be a gradual resistance by our lenders to absorb any more of our debt. This will necessitate the raising of interest rates to lure them into investing more of their money. Like the junk bonds of failing corporations, which promise great returns, if they can ever be redeemed, our promissory notes will be looked upon with a great deal of skepticism. As our debt grows larger, and the servicing of the interest becomes a greater burden upon our budget, our lenders will began to question whether we can repay our obligations, and if we do, what kind of deflated value will they be worth.

As the supply of new investment dollars begins to dry up, the government will be forced into the further plundering of any money still available in trust funds. There also will be an increased taxation of the middle class to shoulder more of the national budget—the poor and the ultra rich will be left largely untouched. Then will be the selling of any hard assets we possess—gold, foreign holdings, land, military hardware, and anything deemed valuable. What will be left of America will only be an empty shell of our former glory. Like Israel's demise when its enemies began to plunder them, so will be the end state of America.

2 Chr 36:11-19 Zedekiah was one and twenty years old when he began to reign, and reigned eleven years in Jerusalem. And he did that which was evil in the sight of the LORD his God, and humbled not himself before Jeremiah the prophet speaking from the mouth of the LORD. And he also rebelled against king Nebuchadnezzar, who had made him swear by God: but he stiffened his neck, and hardened his heart from turning unto the LORD God of Israel. Moreover all the chief of the priests, and the people, transgressed very much after

all the abominations of the heathen; and polluted the house of the LORD which he had hallowed in Jerusalem. And the LORD God of their fathers sent to them by his messengers, rising up betimes, and sending; because he had compassion on his people, and on his dwelling place: But they mocked the messengers of God, and despised his words, and misused his prophets, until the wrath of the LORD arose against his people, till there was no remedy. Therefore he brought upon them the king of the Chaldees, who slew their young men with the sword in the house of their sanctuary, and had no compassion upon young man or maiden, old man, or him that stooped for age: he gave them all into his hand. And all the vessels of the house of God, great and small, and the treasures of the house of the LORD, and the treasures of the king, and of his princes; all these he brought to Babylon. And they burnt the house of God, and brake down the wall of Jerusalem, and burnt all the palaces thereof with fire, and destroyed all the goodly vessels thereof.

When every legitimate measure to further finance our extravagance fails, there will be no recourse but to print money that has no value attached to it. At this point the scourge of hyper-inflation will make our currency worthless. Like Germany before World War II, when it took a wheel burro full of money to buy a loaf of bread, so will our economy be plunged into chaos.

Rev 6:6 And I heard a voice in the midst of the four beasts say, A measure of wheat for a penny[33], and three measures of barley for a penny; and see thou hurt not the oil and the wine.

Those on fixed incomes, such as retirees, will suffer the worst. While everyone, except the rich, who are **"the oil and the wine,"** will find it very difficult to survive. At this point society

---

[33] A penny equaled a day's wages when this prophecy was written.

will break down and anarchy will begin to reign. In this nation, where everyone has had bread to the full, and many rely upon government handouts to meet their needs, or think the government owes them a living, it will mean a time of increasing crime and violence. People will have no qualms about how they find the resources upon which to live. Because many Americans no longer fear God, or have any moral restraints against doing what is necessary to survive, there will be looting and rioting on a scale we have not witnessed as yet.

Psalm 36:1 The transgression of the wicked saith within my heart, that there is no fear of God before his eyes.

Furthermore, when our money becomes worthless, we won't be able to pay for the armies of police and National Guard which now hold lawlessness in check. The justice system will no longer be able to deal with the increase in violent offenders, and the prison populations will be bulging, if they are even operational. America's future landscape will look much like the apocalyptic movies that have been produced, except it will be real. Gangs will roam the streets, while law abiding citizens will be imprisoned in their own homes, and forced to defend themselves.

Does all of this seem to be an unlikely scenario, or, "it can't happen in America"? Why do we think we are any different than the other countries around the world that go through these political and economic upheavals all the time? Now that America has abandoned the True and Living God, and now lives as if there is no God, we will fall prey to the same fate as any other heathen nation. We have already had a foretaste of this in America when we witnessed the riots which broke out in many of our major cities; and we stood aghast as looting and burning took place with no means to stop it. These so-called "race riots" were nothing more then an excuse for men to carry out their unbridled desire for evil. Think of what will happen when millions of people can't find enough food through legitimate means.

Psa 9:17 The wicked shall be turned into hell, and all the nations that forget God.

Added to America's economic collapse will be a complete moral breakdown. Although we already see the evidence of where we are heading, this will not compare to our future state, when all restraints that hold back the evil desires of men are removed. Drug use, alcohol abuse, sexual deviancy, and other taboos will flood our country as society will no longer have the resources to maintain decency and order. When men and women, who no longer are bound by the fear of God or the morals of society, are allowed to freely and openly express their wanton desires, America will be inundated by **"abominable filth."** Most people are content to abide morally and lawfully, if their needs are met; but when the future disintegration begins to happen, many of these people will join the ranks of those who seek only lustful fulfillments.

Nah 3:5-6 Behold, I am against thee, saith the LORD of hosts; and I will discover thy skirts upon thy face, and I will shew the nations thy nakedness, and the kingdoms thy shame. And I will cast abominable filth upon thee, and make thee vile, and will set thee as a gazingstock.

Finally, America's future state will be a period of great spiritual darkness. In a land where there is a church on every corner, and a Bible in every home and motel room, it seems incredible to believe that we would ever become spiritually bankrupt; but that is the curse for those who have the truth, but reject it, or do not live according to it. Our faith in the God of the Bible, and in the Gospel of Jesus Christ are what made this country great; but society, as a whole, no longer treasures our Christian heritage; and that has led to our downfall. There is coming a day however, when the voices of those who proclaim the truth will be silenced, and God's Word will no longer have any relevance. This country will be sent **"strong delusion"** and believe the lies of the Wicked One. America, like the rest of the world, will one day worship the beast and his father, Satan. We already are beginning to see this happen as we embrace the lies of evolution and the "Big Bang." People scoff at the Bible and ridicule those who are believers. They view the Bible as just a collection of myths, with no modern relevancy; and religion is seen as a crutch, or the "opiate of the masses." The religion of humanism, which is now deeply rooted in American culture, is based upon the very thing that caused Lucifer[34] to fall. Therefore, America has already traveled a great distance down the road to the coming darkness, and only spiritual revival would bring us back.

2 Thess 2:11-12 And for this cause God shall send them strong delusion, that they should believe a lie: That they all might be damned who believed not the truth, but had pleasure in unrighteousness.

1 Tim 6:20-21 O Timothy, keep that which is committed to thy trust, avoiding profane and vain babblings, and oppositions of science falsely so called: Which some professing have erred concerning the faith. Grace be with thee. Amen.

2 Tim 3:13 But evil men and seducers shall wax worse and worse, deceiving, and being deceived.

Isa 14:12-14 How art thou fallen from heaven, O Lucifer, son of the morning! How art thou cut down to the ground, which didst weaken the nations! For thou hast said in thine heart, I will ascend into heaven, I will exalt my throne above the stars of God: I will sit also upon the mount of the congregation, in the sides of the north: I will ascend above the heights of the clouds; I will be like the most High.

---

[34] Lucifer was the arch angel who rebelled against God, and became the Devil, or Satan.

What Can Be Done to Restore the Dream?

America, like so many other great nations, will one day fall from within, if drastic measures are not taken. God's hand of judgment is already being seen upon our nation, and only national repentance will stay His hand. However, what can we, as individuals, do to restore God's blessings upon our land, or to survive the coming collapse? Although each of us has a different sphere of influence as to how we might change America, there are some basic actions, which, if followed, can help prolong America's future, or at least not make us a part of the problem. We may not be able to stem the tide on a national level, but we can help to preserve our own lives, our families, and our neighbors and friends.

- The most important thing that any of us can do is to pray for God's intercession in our nation. Since it was God who helped our forefathers in establishing America; and it was God who blessed this land and made America great; and it is now God who is allowing America to fall—we are only fooling ourselves if we think that we can change America with human, or political reforms. We have already seen the failure of conservative politicians, the Moral Majority, and other political action groups, who have attempted to bring America back to God, or to conservative values. While we don't condemn such endeavors, without God's help and blessings, all such efforts will fail. Consider what the following verses put forward about what we say.

2 Chronicles 7:14 If my people, which are called by my name, shall humble themselves, and pray, and seek my face, and turn from their wicked ways; then will I hear from heaven, and will forgive their sin, and will heal their land.

1 Timothy 2:1-2 I exhort therefore, that, first of all, supplications, prayers, intercessions, and giving of thanks, be made for all men; For kings, and for all that are

in authority; that we may lead a quiet and peaceable life in all godliness and honesty.

Psalm 127:1 Except the LORD build the house, they labour in vain that build it: except the LORD keep the city, the watchman waketh but in vain.

- As individuals, and as a nation, we must turn our dependence back upon God. All of our false dreams were idols that caused us to turn from the true God. When America began to look to its own resources as our strength and security, we became idolatrous. When we began to look to the gods of democracy, freedom, wealth, and military might, we began to worship the blessings of the Creator, instead of the Creator. America has become so blinded by its pride that it no longer feels that God is relevant, and we have allowed every trace of our Christian heritage to be removed from our government and schools. God will continue to throw down all of these false images until we are either destroyed or we turn our hearts back to Him. We cannot make this choice for others, but we can influence others by making it for ourselves.

Jeremiah 2:11-13 Hath a nation changed their gods, which are yet no gods? but my people have changed their glory for that which doth not profit. Be astonished, O ye heavens, at this, and be horribly afraid, be ye very desolate, saith the LORD. For my people have committed two evils; they have forsaken me the fountain of living waters, and hewed them out cisterns, broken cisterns, that can hold no water.

Joel 2:12-13 Therefore also now, saith the LORD, turn ye even to me with all your heart, and with fasting, and with weeping, and with mourning: And rend your heart, and not your garments, and turn unto the LORD your God: for he is gracious and merciful, slow to anger, and of great kindness, and repenteth him of the evil.

Joshua 24:15 And if it seem evil unto you to serve the LORD, choose you this day whom ye will serve; whether the gods which your fathers served that were on the other side of the flood, or the gods of the Amorites, in whose land ye dwell: but as for me and my house, we will serve the LORD.

- At the same time that we put our trust in the Lord, we must stop depending upon the false idols of this world. Repentance involves turning from idols to the Lord, and not just adding the Lord to our list of benefactors. The purpose of government was never to provide a welfare system, but to protect its citizenry so that they could live in peace and provide for themselves. As we have already discussed, Federal giveaway programs were only created to buy votes for those in office. America takes from those who work, or borrows against the future of America, and gives to those who want something for nothing. The Bible declares that, **"if any would not work, neither should he eat."** Are there cases where people genuinely need help?—of course. However, those needs are to be met first by their extended families, and then by the people of God. Are there those who are legitimately owed a living by the government, such as those who have paid into Social Security all their lives, or those on military disability or pensions, or those whose work for the government has been in honest and necessary vocations?—of course. But the vast majority of people who draw upon Uncle Sam for their livelihood are only leeches upon society. Here again, if we are part of the problem, then we need to wean ourselves off of government subsidies and turn our dependence upon the Lord.

Barack Obama— *"Our government should work for us, not against us. It should help us, not hurt us. It should ensure opportunity not just for those with the most money and influence, but for every American who's willing to work. That's the promise of America - the idea that we are responsible for ourselves, but that we also rise or fall as one nation; the fundamental belief that I am my brother's keeper; I am my sister's keeper. That's the promise we need to keep. That's the change we need right now."*

Isaiah 30:1-3 Woe to the rebellious children, saith the LORD, that take counsel, but not of me; and that cover with a covering, but not of my spirit, that they may add sin to sin: That walk to go down into Egypt, and have not asked at my mouth; to strengthen themselves in the strength of Pharaoh, and to trust in the shadow of Egypt! Therefore shall the strength of Pharaoh be your shame, and the trust in the shadow of Egypt your confusion.

2 Thess 3:10 For even when we were with you, this we commanded you, that if any would not work, neither should he eat.

I Tim 5:16 If any man or woman that believeth have widows, let them relieve them, and let not the church be charged; that it may relieve them that are widows indeed.

- Over the last four decades, most Americans, including many of God's people, have been lured into believing that the accumulation of wealth would provide for them financial security. We have seen a proliferation in IRA's, annuities, stocks, bonds, and other investment vehicles designed to let the average American retire in comfort. For a while these schemes seemed to be delivering on their promises, as millions of Americans started to accumulate sizable nest eggs. Dreams of retiring rich were within the reach of many; but like all dreams, they vanished with the bursting of the tech-bubble, September 11th, the housing crash, and the recession that followed.

God provided for the nation of Israel on a daily basis. The mania which fell in the wilderness could only be stored for one day, but then began to rot. The Lord's model prayer for His disciples also affirmed this principle— **"Give us day by day our daily bread."** We don't need large bank accounts or retirement nest eggs for our futures to be secure. We need to serve the Lord and walk by faith, believing that He will supply our needs. Everything else that we depend upon are false idols. Is it any wonder that God allowed the attacks of September 11th and the stock market crash to occur? God is jealous over His people, and will not allow them to worship false idols. Those who desire to live the true American Dream must return to the faith of our forefathers, who looked to God for their needs and were thankful.

Exodus 16:2-4 And the whole congregation of the children of Israel murmured against Moses and Aaron in the wilderness: And the children of Israel said unto them, Would to God we had died by the hand of the LORD in the land of Egypt, when we sat by the flesh pots, and when we did eat bread to the full; for ye have brought us forth into this wilderness, to kill this whole assembly with hunger. Then said the LORD unto Moses, Behold, I will rain bread from heaven for you; and the people shall go out and gather a certain rate every day, that I may prove them, whether they will walk in my law, or no.

Luke 11:3 Give us day by day our daily bread.

Matt 6:24-33 No man can serve two masters: for either he will hate the one, and love the other; or else he will hold to the one, and despise the other. Ye cannot serve God and mammon. Therefore I say unto you, Take no thought for your life, what ye shall eat, or what ye shall drink; nor yet for your body, what ye shall put on. Is not the life more than meat, and the body than raiment? Behold the fowls of the air: for they sow not, neither do they reap, nor gather into barns; yet your heavenly Father feedeth them. Are ye not much better than they? Which of you by taking thought can add one cubit unto his stature? And why take ye thought for raiment? Consider the lilies of the field, how they grow; they toil not, neither do they spin: And yet I say unto you, That even Solomon in all his glory was not arrayed like one of these. Wherefore, if God so clothe the

grass of the field, which to day is, and to morrow is cast into the oven, shall he not much more clothe you, O ye of little faith? Therefore take no thought, saying, What shall we eat? or, What shall we drink? or, Wherewithal shall we be clothed? (For after all these things do the Gentiles seek:) for your heavenly Father knoweth that ye have need of all these things. But seek ye first the kingdom of God, and his righteousness; and all these things shall be added unto you.

Rom 1:17 For therein is the righteousness of God revealed from faith to faith: as it is written, The just shall live by faith.

Phil 4:19 But my God shall supply all your need according to his riches in glory by Christ Jesus.

Exodus 34:14 For thou shalt worship no other god: for the LORD, whose name is Jealous, is a jealous God:

- One of the major issues that many Americans face today is that of health care. This is also another area where we have become idolatrous. Although prayer and looking to God for our healing ought to be the first thing we do, few people will unless the doctor says there's nothing more he can do. God is not impressed when we put Him last on the list of who we call upon for healing. We have the greatest (and most expensive) health care system in the world, but Americans have among the highest rates of heart disease, cancer, and diabetes found anywhere. I believe this is also an area where we may be experiencing the judgment of God. When our security lies in having health insurance to provide for our medical care, we make it an idol. When doctors, drugs, and hospitals are the first things we look to for our healing, we make them an idol. I am not saying that God does not, and cannot use these things as aides to our healing, but our trust must be in Him. If we don't have health insurance, we still have God. If we don't have access to medical care, we still have Him. Many of our forefathers lived long and healthy lives without the massive health care system we have created in America; and we are much more knowledgeable about what it means to have a healthy lifestyle.

However, many of our health problems are the direct result of our disregarding a healthy lifestyle. We eat the wrong foods, we don't exercise, and we entertain bad habits that provide us with only momentary pleasures. Are we sick or have physical problems, then we should ask God for His wisdom to know what to do. Maybe a change in our lifestyle is what is needed, or maybe a doctor's advice and care is needed, in either case we need to depend upon the Lord. Are we addicted to alcohol, cigarettes, drugs, or even over-eating, then we must look to God for our deliverance. Many of our health related problems can be solved without expensive treatments.

Our nation has now instituted a national health care program that promises to provide for the needs of every American; but it will only be another massive program that will sink us deeper in debt and provide little benefit in return. It is only another government sponsored, humanistic approach to solving our problems. Although national healthcare has been the dream of many, it will only create yet another bureaucratic nightmare. As individuals we must stop looking to the gods of health care and re-focus our dependence upon the Lord. Am I advocating tearing up our insurance cards and refusing to seek medical attention?—absolutely not. It all comes down to this—who is our god; and what are we trusting in?

Exodus 15:26 And said, If thou wilt diligently hearken to the voice of the LORD thy God, and wilt do that which is right in his sight, and wilt give ear to his commandments, and keep all his statutes, I will put none of these diseases upon thee, which I have brought upon the Egyptians: for I am the LORD that healeth thee.

James 5:14-15 Is any sick among you? let him call for the elders of the church; and let them pray over him, anointing him with oil in the name of the Lord: And the

prayer of faith shall save the sick, and the Lord shall raise him up; and if he have committed sins, they shall be forgiven him.

Luke 8:43-44 And a woman having an issue of blood twelve years, which had spent all her living upon physicians, neither could be healed of any, Came behind him, and touched the border of his garment: and immediately her issue of blood stanched.

The following is a list of practical things we all can do to survive in the days ahead, and maybe help others too. These steps will also help to bring a "grassroots" change to America.

1. Get out of the rat race of making more money so you can buy more things. Materialism and covetousness are sins in the eyes of God. The lust for wealth and things is what has lured America away from God.

1 John 2:15-16 Love not the world, neither the things that are in the world. If any man love the world, the love of the Father is not in him. For all that is in the world, the lust of the flesh, and the lust of the eyes, and the pride of life, is not of the Father, but is of the world.

Luke 12:15 And he said unto them, Take heed, and beware of covetousness: for a man's life consisteth not in the abundance of the things which he possesseth.

2. Stop borrowing and overspending. Try to live free from debt or get out of the debt you are in. There are many good Christian programs designed to help people get liberated from debt. Debt is a sign that we want more than God intends to give us. If your mortgage and car payments have you drowning in debt, pray for an escape. If you are living above your means, try to downsize into a less expensive home or car. Sell the things you don't need and use the money to pay off debts. The only kind of debt that makes any sense is buying a home and getting out of rent payments. However, even this must be done wisely. Many people bought houses when the market had

topped out, and then the bubble burst, leaving them with an investment for which they struggle to pay for or sell. Look for a house that has a potential to increase in value by putting in some "sweat equity." Borrowing to pay for a new car or a high priced used car is almost always a bad decision. There are plenty of good bargain vehicles to be found for which most people can pay cash. Furthermore, don't borrow money to pay for things which are not an absolute necessity. Save up, pay cash, or do without. Our founding fathers lived without many of the things which we consider to be "necessities," and were happier than most people living today who have all the "toys."

Rom 13:8 Owe no man any thing, but to love one another: for he that loveth another hath fulfilled the law.

1 Tim 6:6-10 But godliness with contentment is great gain. For we brought nothing into this world, and it is certain we can carry nothing out. And having food and raiment let us be therewith content. But they that will be rich fall into temptation and a snare, and into many foolish and hurtful lusts, which drown men in destruction and perdition. For the love of money is the root of all evil: which while some coveted after, they have erred from the faith, and pierced themselves through with many sorrows.

3. Learn to live simply with less. Stop paying full price for new clothes when you can buy nice things at garage sales or thrift stores. Cook and eat more meals at home using healthier ingredients. Enjoy simple pleasures like hiking or going to the park. Americans have been lured into thinking that we need to pay a lot of money to be entertained; but what did our forefathers do to make life satisfying? Start a hobby, raise a garden, learn to sew, make crafts, write, or paint. There are many enjoyable things to do that don't cost a lot of money. There are also opportunities to serve the Lord by serving others. Living for others will make our lives rich and rewarding.

2 Cor 1:12 For our rejoicing is this, the testimony of our conscience, that in simplicity and godly sincerity, not with fleshly wisdom, but by the grace of God, we have had our conversation in the world, and more abundantly to you-ward.

4. The early pioneers were known for their helping one another. Even today the Amish and Mennonites are community minded, and work together to support their neighbors. In a time when most Americans don't even know who their neighbors are, we need to reach out to those in need. We need to recreate the spirit of brotherly love that once existed among our people. The government needs to get out of the welfare business and let churches and individuals do that work. We would all pay fewer taxes, and those who are legitimately in need would be better taken care of, if we would love our neighbor as ourselves.

William Clinton—*"We need a spirit of community, a sense that we are all in this together. If we have no sense of community, the American dream will wither."*

Luke 6:38 Give, and it shall be given unto you; good measure, pressed down, and shaken together, and running over, shall men give into your bosom. For with the same measure that ye mete withal it shall be measured to you again.

Prov 19:17 He that hath pity upon the poor lendeth unto the LORD; and that which he hath given will he pay him again.

Gal 5:14 For all the law is fulfilled in one word, even in this; Thou shalt love thy neighbour as thyself.

5. Pray for and support political reform in America. We need to make our voices heard by those in office that we want less government, a balanced budget, and an end to the Federal giveaways. The major political parties each have their own agendas, and neither has shown any serious concern about

America's future. A real change is necessary if we have any hope that our children and grandchildren will enjoy the freedoms and liberties of the past generations. Each of us must pray for God's intervention in America, and seek His face as to what we can to do to save our country.

Thomas Jefferson—*"The price of freedom is eternal vigilance."*

William Henry Harrison—*"A decent and manly examination of the acts of the Government should be not only tolerated, but encouraged."*

Job 12:18-23 He looseth the bond of kings, and girdeth their loins with a girdle. He leadeth princes away spoiled, and overthroweth the mighty. He removeth away the speech of the trusty, and taketh away the understanding of the aged. He poureth contempt upon princes, and weakeneth the strength of the mighty. He discovereth deep things out of darkness, and bringeth out to light the shadow of death. He increaseth the nations, and destroyeth them: he enlargeth the nations, and straiteneth them again.

6. Get involved with the Lord's work in America. Too many of God's children are sitting on the sidelines and watching our country disintegrate. Many Christians are not even counted faithful in attending worship services; and most do not use their gifts and talents in promoting the Gospel message. Believers who are not serving the Lord will have no one to blame but themselves if America falls. Unbelievers are in darkness as to what is happening in our country, and only God's people have the light to show them the way to God and truth. Those whose purpose is to destroy America's Christian heritage are hard at work, and as believers we must raise the standard of truth against them.

Heb 10:25 Not forsaking the assembling of ourselves together, as the manner of some is; but exhorting one another: and so much the more, as ye see the day approaching.

1 Tim 4:14 Neglect not the gift that is in thee, which was given thee by prophecy, with the laying on of the hands of the presbytery.

Matt 5:15-16 Neither do men light a candle, and put it under a bushel, but on a candlestick; and it giveth light unto all that are in the house. Let your light so shine before men, that they may see your good works, and glorify your Father which is in heaven.

Isa 59:19 So shall they fear the name of the LORD from the west, and his glory from the rising of the sun. When the enemy shall come in like a flood, the Spirit of the LORD shall lift up a standard against him.

Modern Americans now find themselves in a situation that is becoming more and more like our ancestors experienced in Europe, before they came to this continent seeking liberty and freedom. We now have a new ruling class enthroned in the rich hierarchy, and in our nation's capital. Through taxation and governmental restraints, it has become difficult for the average American to have their own business and to prosper; laws and restrictions are taking away individual freedoms; and worst of all, we have a new state church that is actively working to destroy our ability to worship and serve our Creator God.

It is once again time for Americans to embrace the true Dream of our forefathers—which is liberty and freedom under God. The enemies of this dream are firmly entrenched within our land, and it will take more than human means to overcome them. There must be an awakening in this country that will cause people to turn once again to God, and cry out to Him for deliverance. True freedom begins by turning away from the idols of this world and trusting in God's Son, the Lord Jesus Christ. God is the Author of freedom, and it is only when we are delivered from the bondage of sin, that we are able to experience true liberty. Americans have lost their freedom because we have departed from the faith of the Gospel of Jesus Christ and the teachings of God's Word; but God has not forsaken us, if we will but turn again to Him with our whole heart. Then will the American Dream become a reality once more.

George Washington—*"The time is now and near at hand which must probably determine whether Americans are to be freemen or slaves; whether they are to have property they can call their own; whether their houses and farms are to be pillaged and destroyed, and themselves consigned to a state of wretchedness from which no human efforts will deliver them. The fate of unborn millions will now depend, under God, on the courage and conduct of this army. Our cruel and unrelenting enemy leaves us no choice but a brave resistance, or the most abject submission. . . . We have, therefore, to resolve to conquer or to die."*

2 Cor 10:3-4 For though we walk in the flesh, we do not war after the flesh: (For the weapons of our warfare are not carnal, but mighty through God to the pulling down of strong holds;)

John 8:32 And ye shall know the truth, and the truth shall make you free.

John 8:36 If the Son therefore shall make you free, ye shall be free indeed.

Isa 44:22 I have blotted out, as a thick cloud, thy transgressions, and, as a cloud, thy sins: return unto me; for I have redeemed thee.

Jer 4:1 If thou wilt return, O Israel, saith the LORD, return unto me: and if thou wilt put away thine abominations out of my sight, then shalt thou not remove.

Jer 24:6-7 For I will set mine eyes upon them for good, and I will bring them again to this land: and I will build them, and not pull them down; and I will plant them, and not pluck them up. And I will give them an heart to know me, that I am the LORD: and they shall be my people, and I will be their God: for they shall return unto me with their whole heart.

Other Books Available From This Author:

The Garden and The Gospel

Without a doubt, the two greatest events that have most affected mankind were the fall of Adam in the Garden of Eden and the crucifixion of Jesus Christ upon Mount Calvary. The first event plunged man into the darkness and horrors of sin that have plagued this earth since that time; the second has restored to many of Adam's race freedom from that darkness. In the Garden man lost his innocence, lost fellowship with his Creator, and lost Paradise. On the hill of Calvary the way was opened for man's sin and guilt to be abolished, fellowship with God to be restored, and a future Paradise to be obtained. Because of one tree, man became a fallen creature with a new master, was brought into the bondage of sin, and was condemned to die. Because of the tree of Calvary, many have been made a new creature with a new Lord, have been set free from the slavery to sin, and have the gift of eternal life.

The Words of Job's Wife

Almost everyone is familiar with the story of Job, of how an unseen battle between the Lord and Satan resulted in this man Job losing everything he had, and then being afflicted with a most hideous and painful disease. While most of us may be able to give at least an elementary account of the book, few people really understand what is the deeper message of the story. Although many books and sermons have been based upon the trials of Job, this author has come to believe that the most misunderstood character in Job's story is that of his own wife. To many, her attitude has been likened to that of Queen Jezebel, a Biblical icon of maliciousness; but what kind of woman was Job's wife really; and what may we gather from her rather infamous suggestion for Job to "curse God and die"?

Who or what was behind her seemingly bitter advice to her husband, and was there a deeper meaning to it? Upon her very words therefore is this book based, and is designed to challenge God's people to take another look at Job, Job's wife, and God's purpose concerning Job's suffering.

The Ten Commandments of Grace

There is a great battle going on in the world over the relevancy of the Ten Commandments—as they are presented in the Judeo-Christian Bibles. While the governments of many countries throughout the world have patterned their laws after certain aspects of the Ten Commandments, any attempt to assign to them religious significance, or attach to them their source as coming from God, is vigorously fought against. There is also, even among religious circles, a great debate concerning the meaning and purpose of those ten laws. Many would question the validity of some of those edicts as they might apply to modern day religion. Others would spiritualize many aspects of those laws, while maintaining a firm belief that all of them are still in effect in some form or another. The purpose then, of this study, is to present from an entirely Biblical viewpoint, all of the important aspects, as well as the modern relevancy of those Ten Commandments.

The Purpose of God Concerning Sin

Indeed, one of the biggest issues that we as humans face is that of sin. Still, there are many who question even the existence of sin, preferring to label self-destructive or anti-social behavior as various diseases caused by genetics, or the result of a warped psychic caused by improper parenting. Humanists, atheists, and evolutionists favor this kind of rational because it releases them from any anxieties caused by a belief in God, sin, and judgment to come. Other people, who acknowledge the existence of a Supreme Being, admit that there are evils in this world that cannot be explained away with this kind of human reasoning.

They conclude that there must be some evil force, such as sin, that affects some, and maybe all humans in some way; but they are ignorant of knowing exactly what it is or how to deal with it. Many people therefore, choose simply to ignore the issue of sin, while they spend their lives in material pursuits. Many others adopt various philosophies and religious beliefs that provide a salve for their troubled consciences. Though they acknowledge the existence of God, and of one day possibly seeing Him face to face, they are unsure, or even self-deceived about what will be His response concerning their faults, failures, and sins. The purpose therefore of this book, is to provide in simple terms, the answers to the most basic questions about sin, its consequences, and to present the Biblical solution for this human problem

Ominous Verses in the Bible

Undeniably, no other book that has ever been written has caused as much controversy as the Bible. It has been ridiculed, scorned, censored, outlawed, burned, and generally dismissed as an archaic book with little worth for modern day man. Many view its contents as merely a collection of fairy tales, mystical prophesies, inaccurate historical accounts, and ancient poetry. Skeptics deny its claim of divine inspiration; and instead attribute its writings to religious zealots who were deceived about what they believed and wrote about. On the other hand, millions of other people believe that its message was inspired by God; and they have found within its pages spiritual insight, comfort, and hope. However, if anyone would be honest enough to say so, some verses in the Holy Scriptures also cause us to be uneasy at the least, and morbidly frightened at the extreme. While the Bible gives us reasons for faith, it also gives us reasons to fear; while it gives us reasons for hope, it also gives us reasons to despair; and while it gives us comfort, it also gives us torment. I have to believe, because it has been so in my life, that those who have put their trust in the Living God, and have attempted to assimilate His Word into their lives, that they are almost daily faced with Scriptures that bedevil, vex, and plague their state of well-being. It is for the purpose therefore, of giving some relief to the saints of God from these troubling verses, that this study has been introduced.

Death, Afterlife, and Eternity

Death—no other word invokes in our minds such feelings of ultimate loss, finality, and even fear—but what is death? To many people death is merely the cessation of life, the natural end of all physical organisms. To those who embrace the naturalist's philosophy concerning the origin of life, that is the most logical answer. Natural forces, they say, created our life, and natural forces will reclaim that life. To those who embrace evolution, there is no hereafter, no reincarnation, no resurrection of life—we merely die and cease to exist. On the other hand, many billions of the inhabitants of this earth believe that there is something beyond the grave to which all earthly life is transfigured. While there are thousands of variations of beliefs, this book examines death using the only time tested and reliable source of information we have—the Bible. From God's Word we can find the answers to these and other questions: What is death? Why is there death? What happens after death? Is there any hope for eternal happiness beyond the grave?

Who Was John the Baptist?

One of the great enigmas in the Bible is that concerning John the Baptizer. While the physical aspects of who he was are quite apparent from the Scriptures, the spiritual aspects are ambiguous. We know that he was the one who was ordained to "Prepare … the way of the Lord," "to make ready a people prepared for the Lord." There is, however, another aspect of John's identity that is often overlooked. On at least two separate occasions Jesus indicated that John was more than just

d

someone who was born to be His forerunner. This short study not only examines many of the details of John's life, but also attempts unravel the mystery about who he really was. Finally, by using the example of John the Baptist, this book also looks at how the Faithful God fulfills His promises and purposes despite having to deal with unbelieving man.

Sources of Materials

These books and other materials are available for free online viewing at "http://GodsPurposes.org"; or both the printed and electronic versions are available from this author or at some online retailers. Contact the author for more information.

The Garden and the Gospel

ISBN-10: 1463620411 / ISBN-13: 978-1463620417

The Words of Job's Wife

ISBN-10: 1461182808 / ISBN-13: 978-1461182801

The Ten Commandments of Grace

ISBN-10: 1466282185 / ISBN-13: 978-1466282186

Death, Afterlife, and Eternity

ISBN-10:146628854X / ISBN-13: 978-1466288546

Ominous Verses in the Bible

ISBN-10: 1466330732 / ISBN-13: 978-1466330733

The Purpose of God Concerning Sin

ISBN-10: 1466330686 / ISBN-13: 978-1466330689

Who Was John the Baptist?

ISBN-10: 1470002280 / ISBN-13: 978-1470002282

Printed in Great Britain
by Amazon